From Shelter To SERVICE DOG

A Practical Guide To Behavioral Rehabilitation

By

Rick and Heather Dillender

AFPDT

A FRESH PERSPECTIVE DOG TRAINING

www.afreshperspectivedogtraining.com

From Shelter To Service Dog

A Practical Guide To Behavioral Rehabilitation

ISBN-10: 0989381609

ISBN-13: 978-0-9893816-0-4

Ebook versions are available in several formats from many online retailers.

A FRESH PERSPECTIVE DOG TRAINING PUBLICATIONS

Table of Contents

Dedicated to Tug, Jackson, Kita, Hoshi,
Ted and Khorii
for making all the work worth it.

ABOUT THE AUTHORS

Rick and Heather Dillender are the owners of A Fresh Perspective Dog Training in Albuquerque, NM. They specialize in behavioral rehabilitation for severe problems such as fear, aggression, neurotic fixations, hyperactivity and other negative issues. They have also adapted their methods to a unique system for teaching individuals to self-train service animals for many forms of disabilities, including both combat and non-combat PTSD and traumatic brain injuries, epilepsy, autism, mobility needs, diabetes, and other forms of cognitive and physical impairment. Their system is capable of rehabilitating behavior to allow for dogs to be taken directly from shelters and rescues and with just a few months of training be put into work as service animals.

Rick and Heather provide training and support for a wide variety of no-kill animal shelters and rescues in their area, and have developed programs for shelters that allow for rehabilitation of behavior in dogs on a large scale. They have also trained therapy dogs for a number of programs including childrens' literacy, classroom education and visiting assisted living facilities. In addition to their individual clients they are active lecturers about their methods and approach and they offer an instructor training program and certifications in their system.

Before devoting themselves to working with dogs full time Rick worked for several years as an educator and administrator in post-secondary vocational education colleges and Heather worked as a certified workplace and family conflict mediator. Rick and Heather currently live in Rio Rancho, NM with their adopted daughter and several dogs, including their two service animals.

DISCLAIMER

Choosing to own a dog means taking responsibility for them and the things they do. In this book we have presented our approach to behavioral rehabilitation and for creating a healthy bond, but you as the owner are responsible for how things go. We would like nothing better than to be able to coach every dog owner who reads this book directly to ensure they apply the information correctly and for best effect, but unfortunately that's not realistic. As such, we can't assume any liability for the success or failure of your efforts with your dog and we are not liable for any damage, injury or loss that may arise due to the application of our approach or information.

If you do not feel that you can safely and effectively implement this or any other training regimen or you are simply unsure how to proceed, then you should seek competent assistance from a trainer that has experience working with your particular issues. Never forget that when working with animals you should ALWAYS put your safety and the safety of others first, and it is best to make conservative choices and not take chances with your dog's behavior. It is up to you and no one else to regulate and control your dog.

INTRODUCTION

This book is about how to live with dogs. Specifically, how to deal with the sorts of issues that dogs tend to develop and how to set healthy patterns in their lives to prevent problems from arising in the first place. Our journey into understanding the nature of dogs began a number of years ago when we adopted three dogs that had severe behavioral issues. As a group they had dog aggression, small animal aggression, fear of people, lack of early socialization and destruction at a level we rarely see in peoples' homes. We lost whole rooms of carpet (they would dig a small hole, then go diving for the foam pad under the carpet and drag it out through the hole. We'd come home to a 12 hole in the rug and a sea of blue foam spread throughout the house). They were digging holes in the drywall and ripping out the fiberglass insulation – things were pretty bad.

One of the dogs was so reactive to other animals that if she saw another dog or a small animal she would start to yowl and scream and spin in circles on the leash and then redirect at us and clamp on to a leg. It was a really ugly situation, and it went on like this for quite a long time before we started to gain some understanding into why they were behaving the way they were and how we should deal with it.

At the time we had no real experience with dogs, and so we did the same things other people do when faced with behavioral issues. First of all, when we thought,"our dogs need training" we started teaching obedience. Sit, stay, down, come – we weren't exactly sure what we were trying to get at or how this helped all the other issues, but it's what people do so we did it. We tried all the different training methods we could find to try and find something that they would respond to. We tried treat training, clicker training, the old force methods with choke chains and whatever else we could find with no success. Oh, their obedience skills were stellar. Our dogs were rock-stars at performing specific tasks but as soon as the command was over they were back to ripping holes in the drywall and attacking strangers again.

It finally dawned on us that the issues we were having had nothing to do with obedience skills, so we started doing research to see what information was available for modifying behavior. After an exhaustive survey of all the information we could find we were feeling despondent about it all. There were lots of tidbits of advice available for trying to address individual issues, but it all boiled down to developing work-arounds for the problems and conditioning aversions rather than actually resolving anything. Whether it was squirting them with water or throwing cans of coins and chains at them (really. It's called the "invisible hand" method and as best we could tell it seems to entail mostly just throwing things at the dog. We couldn't make ourselves do that one), there was lots of advice on how to recondition individual behaviors but no real answers. No one seemed to have a comprehensive explanation for how their advice fit within a larger system of understanding of behavior or why the problems existed in the first place.

The underlying premise of it all seemed to be an idea that dogs are just a bundle of conditioned responses and whatever they happen to have done in the past is what they will do in the future. The follow-on to that idea is that if you can just condition them enough, you can work around issues and find some compromise with the dogs' behaviors that you can live with. Whether the advice is to bait the dog away from others with treats or to put mousetraps around the trash to scare them away, the premise is the same – just condition them with either positive or negative reinforcement and the issues will stop.

The one piece of advice that seemed to be pretty consistent was that exercise would address the issues, so we walked our dogs for 2-3 hours every day and taught them to run with a bicycle so we could run with them several days a week as well. The exercise did drain energy off them for a little while at a time, but it seemed that no matter how much we exercised them as soon as they had a nap they were right back at it. We ended up dedicating every spare second we had to exercising them so that we could have a little sliver of calm in the house every now and then. We were killing ourselves trying to keep up with them and all we were really doing was creating super-athletic dogs with continually increasing strength and stamina. It soon became apparent that this wasn't solving anything either, other than just suppressing the issues to some extent.

This overall approach of tiring them out and conditioning around the problems didn't work any better than obedience training to address the problems. The things we used treats to try and deal with the dogs fixated on even more, and the negative stimuli (the choke chains and prong collars, for example) just made them more neurotic, which was absolutely heart-breaking.

When we started to see issues getting worse rather than better from all this, we decided to back up and start over. We began with a very basic premise – dogs in nature don't exhibit behavioral issues. A dog living in the wild with a bunch of other dogs doesn't destroy the den, mess in the den, turn on the other pack mates for no reason, bark and whine obsessively, fixate on light and shadow or any of the other things we were living with every day. Dogs exhibit these behaviors exclusively when they live with humans. Why? What is so different about a dog living with humans that brings out these behaviors? It also occurred to us that dogs in nature set rules for each other and regulate each other, but they obviously don't speak to each other or train each other. How do they do it? When we started to ask these sorts of questions it opened up new avenues for investigating the problems. We slogged back into researching things, just sure we had finally hit on an approach that would address our needs. We felt we finally had the right questions, and all we had to do now was look up the answers.

It took a good deal more work with a slowly dawning sense of hopelessness for us to realize that no one seemed to have asked these questions in this way before and no one seemed to have the answers. Actually, that's not quite true. Out of all the study we did we found two authors that seemed to have some insights that were genuinely helpful in formulating answers: Cesar Milan, the Dog Whisperer, in his book Cesar's Way has some really good information about what we as the owners needed to be doing with our attitude, and an author from

Britain named Jan Fennell has some inspired insights in her book The Dog Listener about how to structure a dog's day. These two authors gave us at least a place to start, and the flavor of some of their respective ideas are still reflected in our approach. Although we have evolved our philosophy considerably from this early starting point, we still recommend their materials as additional reading.

At this point, being the sort of people that fixate on a problem until we know it inside and out, we decided that if no one had all the answers we needed we would have to figure it out ourselves. To that end, we began observing groups of dogs wherever we could find them. Whether watching dogs interact at the dog park, wandering neighborhoods for homes with several dogs in a yard with no one home so we could observe their interactions, watching nature documentaries with the sound off so we could observe animal behavior without the perspective of the narrator (you'd be surprised how different the story is) or volunteering at our local animal shelters so we could observe dogs' behaviors under stressful situations, we just started taking notes and video of what we saw without any preconceived notions about what we were watching.

We spent endless hours reviewing the material we collected looking for the slightest gestures of communication between the dogs for clues to what was really going on and eventually patterns began to emerge. We spotted consistent responses to triggers and stimuli, and we began to be able to accurately predict how dogs would respond to their environment in any given situation. We identified the postures and gestures the dogs were taking with each other, and before long patterns of communication began to be apparent. We took all this information and began to deal with our own dogs, and at long last began to get real success in working them through their issues.

The system we have presented here is the end result of all that effort – refined, filtered and shaped by many years of working with clients with a wide range of issues and unique situations. We have found this approach to be effective in addressing behavioral issues of all sorts, and we have an extremely high success rate for the families we work with. So, on we go. Some of what's contained here you will likely never have heard before, and some of these concepts are so far outside how our culture promotes handling dogs that you may have to really think about it for awhile for it all to really make sense. Just try it. In our experience, it takes 30-45 days to reset most patterns of behavior for dogs once you institute this approach. Every situation is unique of course, but generally speaking if you have been diligent and serious about implementing the material presented here then within 4 to 6 weeks you should feel you have much better control of your environment and that things are well on their way to being settled.

WHAT WE LEARNED

For many people, getting things in order with dogs requires shifting some perspectives regarding how dogs communicate and how we go about resolving issues with them. To begin with, dogs have no idea that they are pets. Did you ever consider that? From their point of view they can have just as much responsibility in their environment as you. Also, think about all the sorts of things we teach dogs that are conditioned skills. Sit, stay, down, off, leave it, where to eliminate – anything where we are assigning a word to an action. These sorts of things are useful, and they really are necessary for a dog to integrate into a human environment, but it's important to realize that none of these sorts of things are natural. Nowhere in nature does one dog make another dog sit and stay. These things are not part of a dog's natural set of behaviors, and so by themselves they have no ability to modify a dog's attitude or level of excitement. These things can help a dog learn the rules of a home and can certainly control their individual actions, but resolving behavioral issues generally requires more than that.

So what exactly is a behavioral issue anyway? When people are asked this question, answers that follow are typically things like acting out at strangers that come to the door, hoarding and stealing food, herding the kids, biting grandma, destroying stuff, whining, barking – the list goes on. What do all of these things have in common? It may seem that these are disconnected, independent problems but if the focus is removed from the specific undesirable behavior and the structure of the problem is examined, the vast majority of issues all boil down to a combination of two things: miscommunication and excitement. The dog doesn't understand what you want and is too wound up to cooperate even if they did.

When we first begin working with new clients they are understandably focused on the end behaviors – "My dog digs and chews up my pillows", "My dog lunges at the end of the leash when on a walk," and so on. That's important to know, and you certainly have to know what to do when undesirable behavior occurs but focusing undue attention on the end behaviors rather than the cause is not where long-term solutions are found. When someone describes a dog that jumps, barks, runs away, and bites people we don't see a dog with four problems, we see a dog with four symptoms of one problem. At the heart of all of those issues is miscommunication and excitement.

Regardless of the issue that we're asked to address, we have the same basic objectives for every dog we work with: they all need to become Calm, Focused, and Agreeable. No matter what you're starting with, if you can get a dog genuinely calm, focused on the handler instead of the environment and agreeable enough to listen to what you want from them then you can find resolution to issues. Think for a moment about any dog with problems that you are familiar with. If the dog didn't learn any new behaviors but were more calm and more focused on the humans in their life would their specific actions seem so problematic? Likely not.

How to do you get a dog to be Calm, Focused, and Agreeable? Just like anyone else: by filling their needs. Dogs have needs – many we recognize such as a need for food, shelter and love but we often miss important concerns, such as meaningful social interactions and a sense of safety and order in their environment. As with any individual, not having basic needs addressed leads to stress, anxiety and a tendency for undesirable behavior of some kind. That's true of people as much as dogs.

Once a dog's daily needs have been addressed a large portion of undesirable behaviors simply go away on their own, and those that remain because of some habitual pattern can be addressed more easily. Some things that a dog does are because it is stressed, anxious, hyperactive or fearful and will resolve on their own when calm is achieved, but some are due to humans inadvertently rewarding undesirable attitudes and actions and essentially conditioning the dog to do undesired behaviors. Those issues will not resolve entirely just because the dog calms down.

Reinforcement for negative behavior can be anything from looking at a dog when they whine to giving treats to get it to stop barking at the window. These sorts of issues will persist until the dog is taught new patterns of behavior in each situation. The important thing to understand is that until you can calm your dog down reliably you can't really tell which problems are environmental and which are reinforced behaviors. Focus on daily routine and helping the dogs know in every situation what behaviors you expect rather than just correcting what you don't like. It will change your entire relationship with your dog.

What You Say Is How You Think

Before we get too far along, it might be useful to take a moment to discuss vocabulary and how you talk about your dogs and their issues. To start with, in our training we avoid discussing dogs in terms of dominance and submission. Those terms get used in the dog world a lot, and while the concepts are essentially valid we find them to be very confusing for the humans. When we talk with people about being dominant with a dog, what we seem to get most often is bully behavior: trying to prove they are in charge by overpowering and intimidating the animal – dominating them. That is NOT leadership, and it has nothing to do with filling a dog's need for order and structure. Dogs don't respond to that sort of thing any better than humans do. We also don't discuss in terms of submission. That often has an association of an animal that is fearful or suppressed in some way. That's not healthy either. That's not what's intended with those terms, of course, but that is often the way things work out in practice. So much so that we avoid the terms entirely.

The relationship we are looking to establish is much more like a well-ordered family. The parents are clearly the authority figures, but rule-setting and correction is always tempered with an attitude of nurturing. When the focus falls too heavily on pecking order and hierarchy it can begin to feel like a manager / employee relationship, which is entirely about the employee toeing the line. That can come across to the dog as heavy-handed and limits access to love and affection as motivators for positive behavior.

We also strongly caution our clients about referring to

their dog's issues as if they were part of its personality. Your dog is not a "jumper" or a "digger" or a "biter." That implies that the action is ingrained and can't be addressed in some way. Your dog is exhibiting jumping, digging or biting behaviors, true, but behaviors exist for a reason and are not part of a dog's default personality. It may sound like mincing words, but your attitude toward your dog will have a significant impact on how you handle issues as they arise.

What We Mean By "Structure"

To understand dog behavior you must understand that dogs are inherently territorial, pack-oriented animals and they have a built-in need to have their environment very clearly defined. It seems counter-intuitive to many people but a happy, calm, well-adjusted dog is a dog that doesn't make decisions. They are hard-wired to need to have a sense of place and feel not only affection from those around them but a sense of belonging and protection within their family. For a dog, choice brings stress. They simply don't have the tools to make sound decisions about a human environment. For example, some strangers that come to your door are acceptable but others are unacceptable. A dog doesn't have the means to sort one from the other. Being left to decide how they will react to strangers, where they will sleep, whether they can run outside at night and bark at noises or when they will eat simply puts too much responsibility on them. Having all the little choices made for them helps them be agreeable to you making the big choices as well.

To provide context for what that means, think about a natural dog pack. At the top of the pack there is an authority figure that leads the group. It's the leader that makes ALL of the important decisions. They say where the pack will go, what it will hunt, what its territory is and so on. It's fundamental to dogs to have their environment defined by an authority figure. If the home environment isn't well-defined in a way they can understand it becomes difficult for a dog to know who to take cues from when issues arise.

Many of the families we work with for resolving severe behavioral issues have been struggling with the problems for years, just as we did. They've tried all the quick-fixes, the work-arounds and obedience training and none of it has gotten them any resolution of their dog's issues. They know all kinds of tricks but the one thing they have never learned how to do is to provide calm, gentle, clearly-defined guidance for their dog that addresses the dog's basic needs. Many families are confused when it's suggested that they need structure in their homes because they provide what they see as a very structured environment. They have the dogs sit at the door, do obedience for treats, sit and stay and have release words for meals and other forms of daily routines. These things are generally good and helpful but the point we have to bring into focus is that these sorts of things are structure around what the humans care about, not what the dogs care about. The dog doesn't really care whether it knocks you down at the door or not. That's a human concern.

A home can have quite a lot of rules and still miss the points that will make maximum benefit for creating calm, focused, agreeable behavior in a dog. Once a family gets to the heart of what a dog's needs are other routines become easier to implement, but no amount of rules will help a dog settle down if the rules are around the wrong things. They need calm, consistent direction, and they need you to be more stubborn about things than they are. You must be the reassuring, guiding parent to your dog that is nurturing but expects to be listened to.

Behavior vs. Level of Excitement

Another key concept to understand when addressing issues with dogs is the difference between a dog's behavior (their specific actions) and their level of excitement (how wound up they are while doing those actions). This is one of the most important ideas to wrap your mind around, and understanding this will make everything your dog does make more sense.

An illustration will help clarify the difference. Picture for a moment the average home with dogs. When the family has been gone and walks back into the house the dogs are happy to see them. They are wiggling, jumping and running around, which the humans interpret as acceptable behaviors. The family doesn't see anything wrong with the dogs being glad they are home so they give attention and affection of various kinds to the dogs. It's important to notice, however, that although the behavior is acceptable the level of excitement is very high. The dogs are happy but also excited, and the humans reward that level of excitement as well as the behavior by talking to them, petting and so on when they walk in.

That's all fine and well until a stranger comes to the door. Now, it's barking, lunging and general fussiness, which are clearly unacceptable behaviors, but notice that the level of excitement in that moment is exactly the same as when the family came home.The excitement is about someone walking through the door. Whether you will get acceptable or unacceptable behavior simply depends on who it is. If the family wants their dog to be well-behaved when strangers come to the door then it begins by understanding that how they come and go each day is setting the tone for the level of excitement the dog will have when reacting to others.

Being able to resolve issues with dogs is in part about being able to identify where in the dog's day an unacceptable level of excitement is being unintentionally rewarded. Dogs don't really understand the concept of sometimes, and they aren't good at being wound up in one context but understanding that same level of excitement is unacceptable in other contexts. We often receive calls from families where the father likes to rough-house with the dog as play but the mother is panicked because the dog is knocking over the baby and stealing things from the kids' hands. Once it's made clear what's happening people see the patterns for what they are, but it's not always obvious to families initially where excitement is being generated.

The day to day interactions in the home need to be consistently reinforcing that calm, regulated behavior and attitudes are what's expected. It's not that they can't ever be high-energy (exercise and burning energy are certainly part of a dog's basic needs) but high-energy interactions should have a specific context such as during a game of fetch and should be able to be tuned down once it's time to go back inside and lay around.

To understand more of why this matters lets expand the idea of level of excitement (this gets a bit geeky but it's worth it so hang in there). When trying to make sense of these ideas, it is often helpful to think of a dog's level of excitement on a scale of 0-10. 0 is asleep, 7-10 is lunging, barking, jumping, biting and other unregulated behaviors. 7 is a particularly important point on the scale because that is the point the dog is wound up enough that adrenaline enters their system. At that point, their brain shuts off and all their behaviors are simply reactive. They don't listen to commands and they have to be restrained in some way to snap them out of it. You have likely seen a dog at this level behind a fence spinning circles while barking or jumping all over the furniture when the family comes home or barking incessantly with a repetitive, insistent tone. Dogs exhibiting reactive behavior are certainly past this point. Perhaps a graph would help:

Level of Excitement Scale

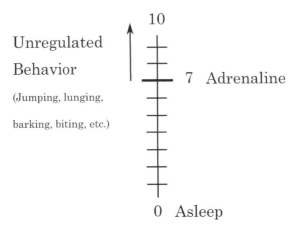

Unregulated

Behavior

(Jumping, lunging,

barking, biting, etc.)

10

7 Adrenaline

0 Asleep

To put some additional values to the scale, understand that the average dog in the average home lives their life at about a 4 on the level of excitement scale. At a 4 a dog can do obedience, make eye contact and generally do what's needed to get along in the home. This works relatively well until there is an excitement trigger in the environment. The mailman comes by, a truck passes, a dog walks by outside, someone comes home or any one of an endless string of things happens that excites the dog. At this point the dog has a rise on the level of excitement scale of 2-3 notches due to the trigger. In other words, in the average home only one thing can happen in a dog's environment before their brain shuts off and their behavior becomes unregulated. Perhaps another graph:

Level of Excitement Scale

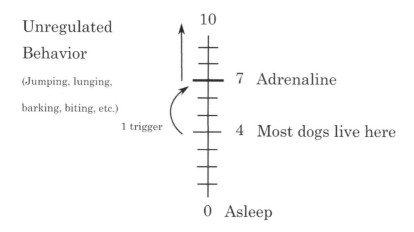

Unregulated
Behavior

(Jumping, lunging,

barking, biting, etc.)

1 trigger

10

7 Adrenaline

4 Most dogs live here

0 Asleep

As you can see, this simply doesn't provide any margin of error to interact with a dog's behavior before they get out of hand. Our goal is to create an environment and daily routines that encourage the dog to have a default level of excitement around a 2. This essentially allows for two triggers to happen in the environment before the dog becomes unmanageable instead of just one. By having the dog calm enough that an initial trigger excites them but they are still able to respond to guidance, it becomes possible to teach them better responses to each stimuli. When they are so wound up that adrenaline pumps into them with every trigger it is impractical to teach them anything new about the situation. They just can't learn when highly excited.

One more concept and this will all pull together. Essentially, the lower a dog's level of excitement the fewer things that count as triggers to begin with. A dog at a 2 needs a trigger such as someone at the door to get excited, while a dog at a 4 is reactive to trucks in the distance, people on the street, dogs they can't see and is generally more alert and jumpy about its environment than is helpful. Bear in mind that as level of excitement increases behaviors intensify. A dog at a 5 is jumping at leaves blowing, acting out at dogs at an extreme distance, and is likely to develop all sorts of peculiarities that owners find confusing. All of a sudden my dog is afraid of rubber boots, my dog is afraid of men in blue hats or whatever. They pace, whine and show a general sense of unease. This pattern progresses as excitement rises.

Owners drive themselves crazy chasing around after triggers, but if you condition a dog not to bark at the fence in the backyard or ignore dogs on the walk without also lowering the dog's level of excitement they will find some other way to vent their excitement and stress. They may start digging or chewing or any number of other negative behaviors but dogs will always vent stress. In the big picture of resolving problems the particular trigger isn't all that important. What's important is that the dog's level of excitement is too high. All sorts of things can be triggers depending on the dog, but regardless of the symptoms the dog is exhibiting the answer is always the same: calm the dog down. One more graph to illustrate:

Level of Excitement Scale

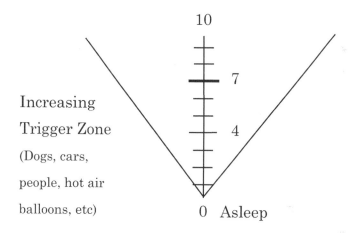

For many issues with dogs, simply calming them down can significantly reduce the severity of the situation and make resolving habitual patterns much easier. A dog with a very low level of excitement is easy to communicate with and easy to teach. The more wound up a dog is, the harder it is for them to focus and be agreeable. It is true that behaviors that start out as reactive can become habitual and still need to be specifically reconditioned, but that is also much easier to do once the dog has a lower level of excitement.

One additional point: don't try and judge a dog's level of excitement by what they do when nothing is happening. Even a very wound up, reactive dog can lay around in a quiet house. Level of excitement is measured by how fast a dog escalates when there is a trigger. For most dogs that's a very different assessment.

A DOG'S NEEDS

What are a dog's needs, anyway? Aside from the specific categories listed below, dogs have a fundamental need for a stable, calm, harassment-free home to live in. Take for example the negative behaviors of the stereo-typical "little dog": barking incessantly, snapping and growling at people and running around in a frenzy at every sound. Despite appearances, small dogs are not inherently different from big dogs. They are, however, treated differently. They tend to be handled and carried and touched entirely too much for their own comfort, and they develop a sense of not feeling safe in their environment. At some point along the way they learn that growling and snapping make people stop touching, and it becomes their go-to tool for controlling the actions of others.

A dog should have an environment that allows for a sense of safety and stability. Corrections should be calm, gentle and always the minimum necessary to get the point across. Praise should be sincere and ongoing challenges such as children, other pets and unregulated adults should be moderated.

A dog can't be more calm than its environment, and the humans do have to set the tone by being calm in their interactions with the dog. It's important to understand that the lack of yelling does not equate to calm. It's a good place to start, since if you are yelling then calm is definitely not happening, but by itself that's not enough. This process requires a somewhat deeper level of emotional control, not just keeping your frustrations and anger to yourself.

The reality is that with a dog you can't really fake it. A dog's senses are so much sharper than ours that they can't be fooled about your state of mind. This becomes apparent when working with service dogs – they know when a person is about to have a panic attack, when blood pressure goes up, when blood sugar drops, when an epileptic seizure is coming and they can detect any number of other things about us. The amount of information they pick up off us is truly amazing. Where we run into problems is that they know how you feel, but they don't often know why.

For humans, most of our stresses and worries come from the past or the future. We're thinking about what we've done or what we're going to do, and our state of mind often doesn't correlate with what is going on around us in the present. A dog, however, lives entirely in the present. They take our state of mind and try to make it fit with what is going on around them. Since nothing is usually wrong in the present, there is nothing for the dogs to direct the stress they are picking up from us towards. Instead, they store it up and pump up their level of excitement, and when there is any trigger at all in their environment they vent it. "There's a dog outside, that must be the problem!", "There's someone at the door, that must be it!", "The kids are running around, that's gotta be it!" and all that stress they have been picking up from us all day comes out in an explosive rush of unwanted behavior.

Some dogs will also vent the stress we create for them by digging, chewing, tearing things up, barking obsessively, whining, fixating on light and shadow and any number of other negative ways. Dogs are individuals and the way they vent stress varies, but the source of the stress is usually the same – lack of understanding from the humans about how our state of mind and our actions affect them.

As mentioned previously, when working with behavioral problems, we try not to focus too much on what the end behavior is. In all situations we have the same goal: for every dog we work with to be calm, focused and agreeable. Plainly put, if a dog is genuinely calm, focused and agreeable then nothing is hard to fix, and if they are not then nothing is getting fixed at all. That being the case, calm has to be the foundation on which all other interactions are built. Bear in mind, though, the dog can never be calm first. Either the humans lead by example with their attitude or calm isn't going to happen.

Picture this scenario – a dog is laying around the house on an average day and the mailman comes to the door. The dog fires off charging at the door or the windows, barking like crazy, scratching at the screens and making a huge, embarrassing scene. How do people typically react? They run to the door pulling at the dog to get them away while yelling for them to "shut up! Shut up! SHUT UP! Quiet Muffy! OFF, OFF!"

Have you ever seen something like that? Well, the dog will never think the human is upset because of them. That would make no sense because everything was fine until the trigger happened. Then, they're just as upset as the dog so the new thing must really be a problem. It sounds almost too simple, but if a person can't manage to be calm about the mailman coming to the door, how can they expect their dog to? The humans must lead by example with their attitude, which means staying calm when there are issues in the environment.

It's true that once the dog has a habit of charging the door then a leash might be necessary to teach the dog to walk calmly to the door instead, but the pattern of behavior can't be addressed until calm is established as part of the response.

Much of solving problems with dogs boils down to learning to control the attitude we as the humans bring to it. It's both the easy and the hard answer – the human has to be calm first. So, when you come home from a stressful day take a few deep breaths before you walk in the house. If you need to have a stressful conversation on the phone or with another family member then put the dog in another room or go for a walk and use your cellphone, but one way or another start paying attention to what stress the dog is being exposed to day by day.

Also bear in mind that it's not just you, it's your environment. If you know that your kids have an hour of running around crazy when they get home from school then that's a good time for the dog to be doing something else so they won't soak up all that little kid energy. When you have company over, be aware of how the unusual activities will affect the dog. What do you think is the busiest week of the year for calls for behavior issues for our business? You might say Fourth of July or Christmas, but no. It's the week after Super Bowl Sunday. Dogs have no idea why all those strangers are packed in the house jumping around and screaming, and they get overwhelmed and act out. Not only that, but the dogs acted out in front of everyone the person knows so the dogs' problems become a priority.

Never forget that dogs will always soak up the stress and excitement in their environment and give it back to you in the form of some negative behavior. You can't always keep your environment calm, but you can pay attention to what your dog is exposed to. It's always preferable to keep them away from situations that they aren't prepared to be successful in.

Getting Down to the Nuts and Bolts

Other than a basically stable environment there are really only four categories of things that dogs care about, and anything that affects their default level of excitement is in one of these categories. They are:

- Food, and how it's handled.
- Social Interactions (including Play, Exercise, Work, Affection and Reunions).
- A sense of Safety in their environment.
- A clearly defined Social Order in the home.

Our goal is always to get maximum benefit for minimum effort out of the things we do every day. When any of these particular things happen, either excitement or calm will be encouraged and it's one or the other. These needs are fundamental for a dog, and not giving them adequate focus simply creates an environment that makes for an unregulated attitude and a heightened level of excitement in the dog.

FOOD
(AND WHAT TO DO WITH IT)

Food is of course very important to dogs. Most people are aware that food can be used as a reward for an action (for example you say sit, the dog's rump hits the ground, you give a treat – action has been reinforced). What is usually missed is that food also rewards a dog's attitude and level of excitement. When a dog receives food while excited we are saying, "Good Dog for being wound up." When a dog is allowed to push another dog off their bowl or stare at another dog while chewing a rawhide it says, "Good Dog for being rude and pushy."

Of the four categories of things that dogs care about, food, social interactions, safety and social order, the last two are ideas we build over time for a dog through many small gestures. There is no obedience command that can say to a dog, "feel safe and agreeable NOW." What a dog has to do to get food from me and get my attention, however, are things that the dog wants that I do have direct control over. For those things I can say, "you must be this calm to get what you want." Food and attention are some of the few levers we have to directly teach an appropriate level of excitement. To that end, there are several rules that should apply to food at all times, and a specific procedure to follow at feeding time. First, what to do.

The Feeding Ritual

We refer to feeding as a ritual because it should ideally be done the same way every time, regardless of who feeds. Consistency and predictability are important to a dog, and steady feeding routines are one of the anchors they hang their understanding of their environment on.

Prep the dog's bowl and put them on leash, in whichever order is easier. Take the dog and the bowl to the couch and sit down with the bowl next to you on the couch or table. Now watch TV, read, do your email or whatever you prefer so the dog can have enough time to calm down. Correct them gently if they try to touch you or the bowl, but other than that just ignore them until they relax and their attitude and level of excitement shift to something calm and agreeable. Just wait them out and they will calm down. It may take awhile at first but it will happen.

Once they lay down, drop their head and maybe give a sigh and it's clear that they have let all the fussy energy go, very smoothly slip the bowl under their nose and let them eat. The idea is to get the food to them without exciting them again. There should be no other formalities than that. No obedience, no release words and no requests for eye contact. For a dog to do any form of obedience they must of necessity re-engage their brain, which will raise their level of excitement from the 2 you finally achieved back to a 4.

Once they have been given the bowl, just let them eat. Many training methods suggest handling the bowl or food while the dog eats to desensitize them to the bowl being touched in the event a child intrudes. Since the dog is never unsupervised around food in our approach those sorts of things are essentially irrelevant for our purposes. It can also very easily undermine trust with the dog. It is the family's job to keep children, other pets and strangers away from the dog while they eat. It's part of what builds the sense of safety that a dog needs.

Once a dog leaves the bowl for any reason simply pick it up and put it away. Whether they finished the food or took one bite and wanted to chew it somewhere else, meal time ends when they leave the bowl. Allowing a dog to come and go from food creates excitement as the meal progresses and will undermine your efforts.

One person can easily feed two dogs this way. If there are more than two dogs we recommend two people be present for feedings so all bowls can be delivered at the same time. Making a dog wait for the bowl while others get food will increase excitement. If you have more than 4 dogs then make a friend who can provide a third set of hands or break the pack down into two groups and feed each group separately. If you must feed several dogs alone, wait until everyone is calm then slip bowls to the dogs that are most likely to wind up again first. It keeps the group as a whole as calm as possible. Distribute the others as smoothly as you can. Not every situation is ideal – just do the best you can to get to the point of feeding genuinely calm dogs. Bear in mind that there is a world of difference between a dog being calm and a dog being still. Calm always has an element of relaxed about it. If the dog is holding still but staring at you intently, they are not calm enough.

It is worth mentioning that safety is always paramount with dogs around food. If you have any concern your dogs are not trustworthy to leave each other alone while eating and afterward, then either attach leashes to heavy furniture far enough apart that the dogs can't engage but can still be fed simultaneously (such as at either end of a couch) or use a crate to contain the most nervous dog. Opening the crate door to put the food in can slow the delivery a bit, but do the best you can. Make sure to re-latch the crate door. If you do not feel absolutely confident controlling your animals around food then you need help from a trainer that has experience working with re-active animals to establish proper safety protocols in your home. Don't procrastinate getting help if you have even periodic safety concerns about your ability to control the dogs.

Feeding Do's and Don'ts

- First of all, never ever, ever leave a dog unattended with food. Ever.

Do not free-feed (leave food down and walk away). Most dogs should be fed twice a day on a regular schedule unless directed to do otherwise by a veterinarian for a specific health reason. There are behavioral issues that start from hunger so don't feed just once a day. Dogs under 6 months or extremely small dogs sometimes can be better off being fed 3 times a day or more for good health. However often you choose to feed, each feeding should be presented with the Feeding Ritual.

- Do not walk away from the dog while it has food. Really.

This also means we don't let dogs wander off and hoard rawhides and chewies, and putting food inside toys and leaving them to entertain themselves is bad. Bad! Bad Owner! Never forget, food always rewards the state of mind and level of excitement the dog has when they receive it. Think about how fixated a dog has to be to get food out of a toy – fuss, fuss, fuss, fixate, Fixate, FIXATE, REWARD! Over and over again, all day long. This creates an unhealthy, hyper-active state of mind that rolls forward to other aspects of the dog's life. For many dogs is the single most destructive thing you can do to their attitude and behavior. Remember how many times your mother told you not to play with your food?

FOOD + TOYS = BAD JUJU.

- No one eats until everyone is calm.

If there are two or more dogs in a home, they need to work as a team at getting along. Since they have to function as a unit, no one is fed until all the dogs are settled and calm.

- If one dog hasn't started eating their meal after being given the bowl by the time that everyone else has finished, remove the food and try again next meal.

No dog should be allowed to wait until everyone else is done, then eat when no one else has any. The dogs are expected to function as a pack and be respectful, which means eating together.

- We recommend feeding dogs inside.

Eating can make a dog feel vulnerable, and adding the additional stresses of noise triggers outside will make feeding a stressful experience instead of a calming one.

- Eating is a primary pack activity, and a dog expects to do it with their pack.

It is important that all the dogs be fed in the same general area at the same time so that they identify each other as pack-mates. As stated earlier, if you are unsure of your ability to control your dogs to safely accomplish this then have an adult present for each dog with the dogs on leash, leash them to furniture, use crates and / or seek professional assistance for your dogs.

- Completely ignore them while they are calming down.

Don't look at them, don't touch them, and don't talk to them. What we're waiting for is for them to calm down, settle themselves, and relax. In this instance, we do NOT tell them to sit or down. This is not the time for obedience commands. A dog can sit on command and still be tense, shaking, or whiny. You can't rush a dog into calming down, and you can't make them be calm by being fussy at them or giving obedience commands. Just ignore them, be patient, and they will eventually settle. Once the dogs get the idea that calm is what's desired, they will calm down faster and faster each time.

- If a dog leaves their bowl for any reason, pick the food up and escort the dog from the feeding area immediately.

We understand that this part doesn't give people warm fuzzy feelings, but it is the part that brings dogs to balance. It makes skittish dogs more trusting, it makes pushy dogs more agreeable – it is one of the most direct gestures available to shift a dog's state of mind.

Think about dogs living in a pack in the wild. Can any member of a pack, except the leader, walk away from food and then come back and take it again? Not a chance. In nature, if you leave food you're done unless you're in charge. Every time a dog is allowed to decide where and when it will eat (even to the point of picking up a mouthful of food and chewing it two feet away on the carpet) it reinforces that the dog has authority over food within its environment which creates problems in other areas. This part must be very diligent. As each dog finishes, pick up the bowls and be done. Also, don't leave empty food bowls laying around. Dogs can still get fussy with each other over the smell of the food that was in the bowl.

- If they don't eat don't try to convince them to.

Not every dog wants to eat every meal, and they may simply not be in a state of mind where they want food. In addition, if you have been free-feeding it may take a few meals for the dog to get hungry. If you place the bowl down and they look at it then turn away or seem uncertain you can jiggle the bowl a little and tell them it's OK, but if after that if they don't show interest just put it away and try again at the next meal. Feel free to make the food more interesting by adding olive oil, plain unsweetened yogurt, a little wet canned food, or other healthy additives to make the meal more enticing, but as long as a dog is healthy they won't starve themselves to prove a point. They will get hungry and they will eat. Stick to the system and it will smooth out.

Treats and How To Use Them

Despite the prevalence of food in dog training, we do not advocate using treats for teaching skills or addressing behavioral issues. Food always rewards a dog's level of excitement when they receive it, and treats tend to make a dog excitable. Not a good combination for our purposes. They also tend to create a dog that fixates on fingers and pockets instead of being willing to make eye contact for approval.

We practice positive reinforcement for training, but it's sincere affection and approval that is the most powerful motivator you have access to. Use it. A dog should do what you ask because they want your love and approval, not because you happen to have a piece of food. If you like giving treats, use them as snacks. Make sure the dogs are relatively calm, then simply give them a treat. Don't over do it, and if you give several throughout the day make sure to reduce the portions at meal time to accommodate so your dog does not develop a weight problem.

SOCIAL INTERACTIONS

Social interactions are the sorts of things that people usu-ally give the most attention to with their dogs. How we give affection, how we play, greetings and other similar things are points in the dog's day that people put lots of focus and energy into, although they don't necessarily get maximum benefit from them. Social interactions are what make a dog feel bonded with a family and are vital for a dog to feel loved. It is also a big part of helping them know they have their own place in the home and are welcome. There is much more to it than many people realize, though, and the area people should have the easiest time with can sometimes become problematic.

At this point, a definition of affection would be helpful. There are five things that count as affection:

- Almost any kind of touching with the hands (NOT hitting, of course)
- Soft eye contact
- Soft voice
- Food
- An approving attitude

Any time a dog receives affection of any kind, they take

it as a reward for their current behavior and level of excitement. This can be really problematic when affection is unintentionally or mistakenly given at inappropriate moments. Unlike with humans, affection cannot lower or redirect a dog's behavior, attitude or level of excitement in any way. It simply reinforces these things. If a child is afraid and they are comforted it will likely make them feel better. If a dog is comforted when afraid it does not help them but rather says, "Good Dog for being afraid." Affection always reinforces things. This one issue is at the heart of many severe problems with dogs. The misuse and poor timing of affection is in fact where neurotic, unhealthy behavior often gets started with dogs.

In particular with fear issues, when a dog has a fear reaction to something and then they receive affection it locks the fear in place. When a dog looks scared and nervous, what feels like the right thing to do is to comfort them. We want to make them feel better, so we give them affection – "it's OK baby, calm down" while we pet them. This seems like the right thing to do because humans are hard-wired to nurture children, and a child might actually get some benefit from being comforted when afraid. However, a child can think about the past and the future, listen to an explanation of why they were comforted and make sense of it all.

Dogs don't speak English (yes, really) and they make simple associations in the present – "Fearful state of mind got me affection. Be fearful more." What we're trying to do is say, "it's OK calm down"; what we are saying is, "Good Dog for being afraid! Be fearful more!" The affection reinforces the fear until it becomes the dog's default reaction to everything.

One of the most common things we hear from new dog owners is, "I'm pretty sure my dog was abused, because he's afraid of everything." Although that's the impression, it's not usually the reality of the situation. Generally speaking, abuse doesn't reinforce fear, it creates aggression. It's affection that reinforces fear. Specifically, affection given to a fearful state of mind reinforces fearful responses. We've gone to many homes where the family has had the dog for its whole life, being gentle the entire time, but the dog cowers and hides in the corner at every noise. What's happened is that every time the dog has a fear reaction someone starts to coddle it. The dog is being loved to death, and it can't improve until the family changes their behavior towards its needs.

We also see reinforcement with affection for reactive behavior. You're probably thinking, "why would anyone give affection to a reactive dog?" Well, when the dog acts out and the owner strokes it saying things like, "it's OK, calm down, stop that..."- that is touching, talking, and eye contact. In other words, that dog is receiving affection for being reactive. It will be reactive again, because the behavior has been positively reinforced.

We see this pattern with hyper-activity, fixation on light and shadow and any number of other negative behaviors. Here's an example of how it often goes: A dog fixates on a flashing light or perhaps the owners use a laser pointer to "entertain" the dog (the horrible things people do in the name of entertainment for their pets...), and while the dog is fixating someone laughs. That's an approving attitude (read affection), which encourages the dog to continue the fixation to unhealthy levels. In that moment the fixation becomes reinforced, locks in place and the dog has essentially become neurotic. We have had clients with dogs that become absolutely fixated on reflections and shadows to the exclusion of all else from only one experience with one of those horrid laser pointer toys.

Here's another example. A dog has reactive behaviors toward another dog out in public, and we grab on and hold it while still allowing the dog to stare and pull forward. That is touching with the hands (read affection) while the dog is being reactive, which encourages the dog to escalate and be even more reactive the next time it sees a dog.

Affection can also be a primary tool for correcting severe issues if it's applied appropriately. Here's an example of using affection properly to shape behavior. A common problem for dogs is being afraid of thunder or fireworks. When the boom happens the dog will likely have a fear reaction to it. If someone gives affection in that moment to try to comfort the dog they would be encouraging it to have more fear of thunder. Instead, they might put the dog on leash and walk it calmly around the house. As the dog is given something else to think about it will start to relax and calm down, and then quiet affection can be shared a little bit at a time to reward the calming down.

It may be just a few moments of self-control for the humans but it makes a world of difference in whether we are making the issues better or worse. No matter how heart-wrenching it may be to not touch, trying to give affection to a dog while they are exhibiting negative behaviors, unstable attitudes or an unacceptable level of excitement will make things worse. You must change their state of mind first, then give love to the healthier attitude.

It's generally a good choice to give affection when the dog is looking you in the eye, when they are calm, when they have just been obedient or when they exhibit any behaviors that you approve of. Remember though, if you pet just because you feel like it without taking into account the dog's current behaviors and attitudes you are simply rolling the dice on whether you will reinforce problems.

Another subtle but important point regarding affection is that the dog will behave however you touch them. If you touch them in excited ways they will behave in excited ways. Make sure your affection is calm, sincere, and doesn't get the dog wound up. To keep a dog calm, touch like you are trying to get a child to go to sleep. If when you pet them their excitement rises, then your affection is too exciting and you should calm your touch. Be loving, be sincere, but don't be excitable.

Reunions

Have you ever noticed that when you've been away from your dog and come back you always get the same greeting, regardless of how long you've been gone? You can be gone all day or just walk to the mailbox and they'll have the same excitable, jumpy behavior when you come back. These moments of greeting are called reunions. Reunions are defined as any time you've been separate from the dog and you come back into the environment.

It's been discussed previously how the interactions the family has each day entering and leaving the home affect how the dog responds to unexpected triggers at the door. At the heart of the issue with reunions is regulating level of excitement. It's absolutely true that your dog is happy to see you and there is nothing wrong with that, but regardless of the dog's intent their excitement is generally very high. No matter how happy you are to see them you should avoid giving them any direct acknowledgment at all until the burst of excitement has passed and they have calmed down. When they have settled down about you coming home and are laying down relaxed, call them to you and give them a nice low-key greeting. Try not to get them wound up again. If they get excited as soon as you give them attention then they haven't calmed sufficiently. Just be patient. As with feeding, once they get the idea they will calm down more quickly but you must be consistent to get the long-term benefits.

Requiring Calm

When we return to peoples' homes for follow-up training, if we don't see the progress we're looking for in calming the dogs then invariably one of two things is happening. Either the dogs aren't being required to be calm enough before feeding or they aren't being required to be calm enough before being greeted during reunions. During these moments either calm is reinforced or excitement is reinforced, and it's going to be one or the other. Be diligent, and be patient. You can't rush a dog into calming down, and you can't make them be calm by being fussy at them. Just wait them out, and they will settle down.

Separation Anxiety

Separation anxiety is a term used to describe a number of negative behaviors such as whining, barking, pacing or destructiveness associated with the dog being isolated. Separation anxiety is created like this: when a family first gets a dog and leaves the house and returns, the dog may or may not notice the coming and going at all. After a couple of days, there is a little tail-wag with a, "hey, it's you" sort of attitude. The family is glad to see bonding start to happen, so they pet right away with a happy greeting. Each day, the excitement of the greeting is reinforced just a little more. Often the family doesn't really notice the rise in excitement because it's so gradual.

After a month or so the excitement has risen to the point that one day the family comes home and the house is gutted. At that point we get a call from a perplexed owner asking how this behavior could have come on all of a sudden -but it wasn't all of a sudden. It was little by little that the foundations for that behavior were laid, and once it gets going it can take just as much time to defuse the stress reactions by handling reunions properly. If you are dealing with separation anxiety in your home, the behavior wasn't created in a day and it won't go away in a day so be diligent and be patient.

Separation anxiety is primarily created and reinforced by how the family enters and leaves the home. When a dog receives affection while they are still wound up and excited during the reunion it reinforces an unhealthy level of excitement. In addition, the anticipation of the high-pitch greeting keys up the dog ahead of time. The stress builds, and as the associated level of excitement increases it vents itself on the house in the form of barking, pacing, whining, destruction, tearing up the door frames, digging at the floors and other negative behaviors.

Set a pattern of ignoring them for a few minutes before you leave and then walk out without any sort of good-bye. When you return be diligent with the reunion procedure and these behaviors will usually taper themselves off.

A Note About Crates and Kennels

Generally speaking, our first piece of advice for families with separation anxiety issues is crating or kenneling the dog while gone if they can't be trusted not to tear things up or if their house-training isn't perfect. However, there are certain things to keep in mind:

- We do not recommend kenneling a dog for more than 4-6 hours without being let out to eliminate, run around and stretch their legs.

If you have to leave them for longer periods consider segregating them in a larger kennel or a single room rather than crate so they can move around. A room with a baby gate across the entrance with a dog door to the back yard may be a workable solution if you are not home for long periods. If you have a dog door but cannot segregate a whole room, consider a very large crate secured on the inside of the dog door so the dog can have access to inside in the event of bad weather but can't roam the house.

- If you keep the dog in a crate, kennel or outside reunions still need to be observed.

When you come in walk up to the crate, kennel or back door and turn your back. When the dog settles down and stops jumping, whining or pawing at the door slowly reach for the latch. If they fire up turn your back again. When they settle down, try again. Keep at it until you can get the door unlatched without them fussing, then open the door and walk away. When the dog is loose in your environment is when the reunion really starts so continue to ignore them until they are calm. If you need to let them out right away to do their business that's fine just don't talk to them, don't touch them with your hands and don't look them in the eye. When you let them back in, the reunion continues until they have settled down.

Dealing With Jumping

Jumping is essentially a territorial behavior. What is a dog really doing when they jump on you? They are trying to take the spot you're standing on. What do people usually do when a dog jumps? They step back, or turn their back (many trainers actually recommend that). Stepping away is giving away territory. They might stop jumping in the moment because they got the affirmation that they don't have to be respectful of your space, but the dog is most likely going to jump on you again later.

When you see a dog get the, "I'm gonna jump on you now" look, instead of giving ground step forward and take the spot they were standing on so they have to move

FROM SHELTER TO SERVICE DOG

for you. Now they have lost territory, which is a real consequence for a dog. Since they didn't get affirmation for the behavior it will stop both in the moment and for the future with a bit of consistency. Don't forget to avoid talking to them, touching them with your hands or looking at them. Just step toward them with a calm, "get out of my personal space" sort of attitude. If they don't get down or try to jump again just take another step toward them.

There is also no need for kneeing a dog in the chest, stepping on toes or pulling their paws up to stretch them into an uncomfortable position to make them have an aversion to jumping. That's mean. Yes, these sorts of things are common advice, but that doesn't make it right. Would you think well of parents that treated children that way?

Play, Social Exercise and Work

Play, Social Exercise and Work all perform the same three basic tasks when used correctly – to increase focus, to build cooperation and to burn energy. It is useful, however, to give attention to each issue separately to understand how to make maximum benefit for minimum effort with your time. Although all three can fill the same basic needs, not every dog wants to do all three. For example, if a dog does not learn to play when young they sometimes don't want to engage with those kinds of activities as an adult. That sort of dog can still have their energies channeled into work and social exercise and feel very satisfied. The goal should be on providing the dog the forms of engagement that best suits their particular needs.

Play

Play can be thought of as high-excitement activities that burn both mental and physical energy. The purpose of play is not only to have fun but to teach the dog how to show self-control and keep their brain engaged even when their level of excitement is high. This is a valuable skill for dogs to learn, and is an important element in regulating challenging behaviors of all sorts.

As such, play should always have some kind of rules. The rules don't have to be very complicated to serve your purposes but they certainly can be. Take fetch, for example. For most dogs fetch means the human gets the ball, the dog sees it and runs down course as the human throws it. The dog gets it, brings it most of the way back, drops it a few feet away and takes off again before the human has the ball back in hand. Or worse, turns the whole thing into a game of keep away. That's not structured play. It doesn't require the dog to think about the activities, engage directly with the human or pause and hold still at any point.

A good game of fetch might start with the dog bringing the ball to the human on command and putting it in their hand. The dog sits and stays as the ball is thrown, then goes on a release command for it. They then bring it back and put it back in the person's hand. If you're thinking that your dog couldn't possibly do that then not only are your expectations for your dog too low but you aren't getting the benefits from play that you could. Of course they likely can't do all that at first, but the process of teaching them will also teach them to focus on you, exhibit self-control, learn some obedience skills and use them reliably. It will promote a relationship that is cooperative and interactive rather than confrontational or indifferent. Does it sound like a lot of work? Sure, but your dog needs that much attention. If they don't get it through positive channels they will get it through attention-getting negative behaviors. See the Appropriate Play section for more information.

Social Exercise

This category is called social exercise because it's not exercise unless a human is involved. Two dogs chasing each other around in circles all day isn't exercise, it's hyper-activity. That sort of thing creates problems; it doesn't help resolve them. Social exercise can be thought of as high-excitement repetitive activities that primarily burn physical energy. Jogging, running with a bicycle and swimming are good examples of social exercise.

Social exercise is an important element in a dog's life and can be a useful tool to help calm issues in the home. It can take the edge off the intensity of a dog's behavior so that all the other calming elements in their life are more effective, but will not substitute for them. It is certainly true that additional exercise can help balance unusual disturbances in the environment, such as when company stays over or the kitchen is being remodeled, but by itself it's not a long-term solution for problems. Dogs need to be exercised both mentally and physically

The main limitations of social exercise are physical issues. Bad hips, arthritis, torn ligaments or any other physical injury will severely limit the amount of exercise a dog can receive and any exercise program for an injured dog should follow a veterinarian's recommendations.

Generally speaking, a dog should receive as much social exercise as health and time permit. Always show moderation, and remember that just because you are a marathoner that doesn't mean your new Bulldog is. Treat their exercise regimen with the same consideration that a new athlete should receive. Not too much at once, not every day and pay attention to any sign of mild irritations before they get worse. In particular, watch the condition of their feet and if you intend to exercise on hard or rough terrain consider shoes for your dog. For animals that can't exercise enough to fill their energy needs focus them instead into work activities.

Work

Work can be thought of as activities with objectives and purpose. It can range from learning to pick up a few toys and put them into a basket to working as a service animal for a disabled person. Work can be low-excitement activities such as obedience training or being a therapy dog visiting the elderly, or high-excitement like competing at agility or learning to find objects or people by scent. The important part is that the activities have some sense of purpose about them. Dogs thrive on having a sense of usefulness and most breeds were originally created to perform work of some sort. Even simple tasks can give a dog a sense of doing something useful which can do wonders to settle a dog's insistence for interaction.

It is difficult to adequately express the value of incorporating a sense of work into a dog's day. Dogs living in the average home are often unfocused, easily distracted, fussy and bored. They express their need for interaction and mental stimulation by making their own jobs which don't usually fit the family's agenda. Guard dog, alarm system, trash grinder, and spokesperson are all dog jobs that don't work well in the home. When the time and effort necessary is put into teaching a dog to do something you genuinely appreciate they perk up and begin to have a sense of satisfaction about their day. They settle into a calm, focused attitude and it becomes easier and easier to teach them new things and redirect their attention when you need to.

A dog's need for a sense of purpose becomes most clear in homes with dogs that fight with each other. A family can institute all the structure in the world, but in most cases the dogs won't finally settle down until each is given a purpose other than fussing at the other dog. It doesn't have to be much but mental stimulation, individual attention from the family, as well as a requirement for a calm, focused and agreeable state of mind can bring a dog along quite far on many issues.

Deciding What To Do

Every dog needs some portion of either play, social exercise or work, and often more than one. The goal is to fill the needs of both the dog and the family. Some dogs don't know how to play or just don't want to, some are unable to exercise and some want very low levels of work. Figure out where the dog's needs and wants are, and then find some way to fill those needs in a way that the family is actually interested in. It's fine and well to decide your Bassett hound should be trained to track game, but if you don't hunt you won't likely keep up the activity. The human has to find the tasks interesting as much as the dog does. Whatever you do, remember that it is important for your dog to have fulfilling activities to look forward to each day.

A SENSE OF SAFETY

Dogs have an inherent need to feel safe in their environment, just as we all do. If their environment seems filled with threats they spend their time on alert, always looking for the next challenge. The miscommunication with the humans generally occurs around what makes a dog feel unsafe. It's difficult for some people to understand how their dog could feel unsafe in their home. The humans feel safe, they provide their dog with plenty of love and have never been the least bit rough with it. Why wouldn't their dog feel safe as well?

To begin with, feeling unsafe isn't just about fearing injury it can be about fearing harassment. Here's an example to illustrate the point: In our own family we have a large group of dogs, ranging in size from a big Rotti-Bulldog mix down to a Pomeranian. The Pom, Ted, has safety issues in our home. Not because any of the other dogs would ever harm him, but he's constantly getting bumped and pushed and jostled by the others. Every time a door opens or the dogs get excited about anything little Ted gets spun around and knocked about. He makes these horribly confused-sounding barks as if to say, "Dudes, really?"

If the situation is left unregulated, Ted becomes increasingly jumpy and barky about anyone moving at all. To resolve his need we have to block the other dogs away from him if everyone gets excited and he usually has to wait and go last through doors and hallways. He gets extra love for sitting by our side instead of running off with the others so he doesn't mind. As we regulate his space for him he calms down and becomes less reactive to everyone's movements.

If you have an older dog and a young dog that gets in their face because they just want to play then you have a dog that feels unsafe. If you have a small dog that gets carried around a lot and who loses their mind at every little noise and snaps and growls at strangers then you also have a dog that feels unsafe. If your dog has become jumpy and growly at your two year old child because they want to give hugs and kisses then you, too, have a dog that feels unsafe.

Notice that all of these situations are about a dog being crowded or touched too much. Just because a dog is tolerant of crowding and touching too much doesn't mean they like it. If a dog drops their head slightly or turns away when approached it is the most polite way a dog can say, please don't do that. Dogs generally give plenty of signals before they get really upset; people just miss them.

Perceived Dangers

Perceived Dangers are the things that a dog can feel threatened by that are external to the home. The mailman, the Fedex guy, the garbage truck, school buses, dogs being walked in front of the house, hot air balloons and just about anything else can act as triggers for a reactive response. We call them perceived dangers because we know perfectly well that most of the things a dog gets upset about aren't real threats. The dog doesn't know that, though, or they wouldn't be upset.

In a moment of perceived danger people tend to either try to correct the dog to make them be quiet or give affection to try to comfort their distress. Neither reaction gets to the heart of the issue for the dog, which is that they need someone to define whether they should feel threatened or not. A dog doesn't have the tools to figure out a human environment, and they need us to tell them repetitively that all the normal activities around the house aren't a problem.

When a dog responds to a perceived danger, whether by being fearful or reactive, completely ignore them. Don't touch them, don't talk to them, and don't look at them. They don't want you to make them feel better or correct them, they want you to make the problem go away. Get up, get between them and the threat (facing the threat, not the dog) and try to figure out what they are upset about. You may or may not be able to identify what the issue is but you should try. Look around, feel calm and positive about your environment for a moment then walk away. If you are calm and confident enough about it the dog will stop barking. Really. Just try it.

This all seems too simple for many people, but think about it for a moment. We are the only translators that our dogs have to make sense out of their environment for them. If the family can't be calm about the fact that the neighbors walk their dog every day and the trash gets picked up once a week then how can they expect the dog to be calm about it? Just stay calm and feel good about the situation and the dog will settle down.

SOCIAL ORDER

Dogs are socially-oriented creatures, and they have an inherent need to understand who sets the rules and solves the problems. Their understanding of where they belong in the hierarchy of the home has a lot to do with how they behave and what sorts of jobs they choose for themselves. When too much focus is brought to the issue of hierarchy and pecking order, however, it confuses the issues rather than clarifying anything. There is so much more in a dog's attitude than just being dominant or submissive. They can be pushy, rude, nervous, happy, satisfied and many other things that can influence how they behave.

Establishing appropriate hierarchy is part of the formula for success, true enough, but it should be a natural consequence instead of a goal. If the family is doing all of the things necessary to make a dog feel safe, feel like they belong, have a purpose and require them to be calm on an ongoing basis then hierarchy will settle itself naturally into a healthy pattern.

All that being said, there are a few points of interest in communicating with dogs that can directly affect how agreeable and respectful they are with the family.

They center around:

-The Walk

-Using an attitude of Possessiveness effectively

-Issues of Personal Space

These concepts help define a family's moment by moment interactions with their dog and the communication that's occurring throughout the day.

The Walk

It seems odd to many people that the walk is discussed here and not under Social Exercise. This is because the walk isn't for exercise. It's for calming the dog's mind and teaching it to pay attention to the handler. When the focus is on going two blocks up and four blocks over so the dog can burn some energy every day, the walk quickly becomes a point of stress and contention with the dog and can deeply undermine the family's relationship. When the goal of the walk is exercise irrespective of the constant ramping of excitement from marching the dog past one trigger after another without good control, the result is a hyper, fixated attitude the moment the leash comes out that turns into unmanageable behavior on the walk.

The purpose of the walk is to build teamwork and co-operation and most importantly to create calm in association with the leash. To that end we always recommend that families spent 2 weeks to a month just walking on leash in the house, backyard and driveway practicing good technique before they attempt to go anywhere or address challenges.

There are several techniques that will teach a dog to walk agreeably by your side. Within our system our preference is for using head halters with a light touch on the leash, similar to working with a horse. A horse is an animal you have to cooperate with, and they don't respond well to being handled roughly. Dogs are no different in that respect. Just because a person can muscle a dog around with chains or prongs or collars doesn't mean they should. In our practice we use an approach for dogs that is conceptually similar to horse training. Just as a horse is controlled with a halter, a dog is also best controlled with a halter. With a head halter a dog can be easily redirected from a distraction or guided through a challenging situation because their line of sight can be controlled.

How the leash is used is also a vital part of the walk. If any tension is held on the leash at all the dog will likely fight and pull against it. The purpose of the leash is to provide guidance and steering, not to hand-brake them in place or restrain them in position. Any flicks on the leash should be light and quick and several very light flicks are far more effective than one hard pull. If the dog paws and fights against the nose strap once it's been introduced, it is usually because the handler is holding tension on the leash. If you are unable to keep the leash loose, find a competent trainer to provide coaching.

No matter what tool is connected at the neck, if it can't turn the nose effectively it can't stop a dog from staring and escalating at another dog or person. We use head halters exclusively with service animals and working dogs in our training programs due to the high level of control needed to work a dog through public spaces. No tool works without proper training and some technique, however. Any tool, including a regular buckle collar, that is misused can cause injury. If you are uncertain about your ability to get your dog to walk calmly by your side without feeling like you need metal tools (chains and prongs), a shock collar or some other device of intimidation then find a competent trainer to help you.

Once the family and the dog can be successful out in public together, walks should be as regular and consistent as possible, always with the intention of fostering calm and control.

Common Misperceptions About "The Walk"

- If I just get my dog enough exercise his behavioral issues will go away

Burning energy off the dog's body is not enough by itself to calm a dog down. It requires far more energy and focus to walk calmly by your side than to pull you around sniffing and peeing on things. Require the dog to think and pay attention and it'll be calm and tired when you get home.

- My dog needs to sniff and roam, and I feel bad if I don't let him wander and sniff around and mark when I walk him

It's true that sniffing and wandering around can be rewarding for the dog, but it should be exactly that – a reward for calm behavior. If you want to let the dog sniff around, then stop walking and let them sniff. You can even change out your regular leash for a retractable leash and give them a 30'-40' circle in which to roam. Stand still or sit down for as long as you like, but when you begin walking again the dog should be by your side on a proper leash paying attention. A dog can only do one thing at a time. He can't follow a scent and pay attention to you at the same time so make sure the activities are separate.

A dog should NOT be allowed to mark on things during the walk. When a dog is allowed to mark territory, they can become more reactive to other animals they encounter, since now all the other dogs are in their territory. Have designated locations to urinate if you wish, but do not let the dog lift a leg on everything they pass.

- I have a big yard / I go to the dog park every day / I have two dogs and they run around together all day for exercise so I don't need to walk them

Having space and running around with other dogs is not a replacement for a structured walk and social exercise every day. Free play creates excitement and hyperactive behavior, while a walk should create a calm, agreeable attitude. It's good for the dogs to have free run and play if it's regulated, it's just not a substitute for a proper walk.

- I live in a cold / hot / humid/ dry/ sunny / dark environment and going for a walk every day isn't practical

It is important your dog gets walked every day, but it is not really important where you walk them. Hooking up the leash and walking around in the house, back yard, or driveway still fills the basic need for the dog to be led through a calm walk. Of course it's better to get your dog out of the house as much as possible, but any walk is far better than no walk when it comes to calming a dog down.

- My dog pulls and lunges at other people / other dogs and I can't take him out

The same principle applies here as above. A walk through the house and backyard is still very beneficial, and it will allow you time to practice walking without any triggers around you. The goal is to build on success, so it's best to practice with reactive dogs in controlled environments before addressing their issues in any case. If you do not feel confident in your ability to safely handle your dog in all situations, seek competent assistance from an experienced trainer who can coach you through gaining control of your dog.

Possessiveness

Learning to use an attitude of possessiveness for communication and control is an unusual idea for many people. It's also one of the most powerful tools available for getting a point across to a dog. If you've ever watched how dogs set rules for each other, a lot of it boils down to possessiveness. It's my ball, my bone, my bed, my toy, my smell, my person, my space, mine, mine, mine. It's like living with toddlers – they're always taking things from each other. It's important to understand that in a natural dog pack the leader is the only one who owns anything. Everyone else is just using the leader's stuff. The leader can take things away, but no one takes things from the leader. The leader feels possessive of everything, including the other pack mates.

As humans we are also capable of possessiveness, but we have social conventions that keep us from having to actually feel the emotion most of the time. It's understood that guests in your home won't handle your drink, touch your cell phone or dig through your underwear drawer. You don't have to sit there the whole time someone is in your home saying, "this is my drink leave it alone, it's my drink leave it alone." However, if you've ever watched a dog guarding a bone you know that they'll lay for hours with an attitude that says, "It's my bone- leave it alone, it's my bone- leave it alone." Tapping in to those feelings is one of the most powerful tools available for defining a dog's environment.

Here's an example of how possessiveness works. In our business we teach group classes as well as private clients. At the first session of a new class cycle we'll have 6-10 dogs in a room all bucking and pulling and biting at the leash. When one of us takes the leash the dog sits down and stops. We hand it back and the dog fires up, and we take it back and the dog quiets down again. It's endlessly frustrating for the families.

Here's what's happening: the moment I take the leash it becomes my leash. It's not the leash, and that dog does not have the right to bite my leash – only because my attitude says they don't and for no other reason than that. Dogs thrive on feeling owned. It's part of what defines safety for them. For the length of time that I'm working with a dog it becomes my dog, because I have the right to say how my dog will behave. I don't have the right to say how your dog will behave, both in my own mind and from the dog's point of view. If I want to convey calm and control to a dog I must also convey possessiveness and ownership in my attitude or they have no incentive to pay attention.

Understand also, possessiveness is how dogs define ownership of things. If a dog is chewing up shoes, pillows, clothes, furniture, the drip system in the garden or anything else, it's because no one has conveyed possessiveness of those things before they were destroyed. It's easy to feel possessive of something after the damage is done ("hey, that was mine!"), but then it's too late. It sends an entirely different message to a dog if the first moment they sniff at something you get in between and back them away with a calm attitude that says, "that's mine, leave it alone." That defines who owns it and the dog will move on to something that hasn't been claimed by someone else.

Rather than putting the shoes and blankets and purses out of reach, we put them in a pile on the floor in the living room and set rules around them. If the dog tries to approach, we get in between and back them away with an attitude that says, that's mine, don't touch it. That defines for the dog what they are allowed to interact with and what they aren't.

Here is another example of how possessiveness works. We provide training for many of the no-kill animal rescues in our area because we do not believe in euthanasia as a solution to behavioral issues. No-kill rescue is a wonderful concept, since once a dog gets into the no-kill circuit they may be passed from shelter to shelter but they're not supposed to be put down. This is a great idea, but when a dog has severe behavioral issues they can sometimes be very difficult to get adopted and get stuck in the system. We are often called in to help those animals.

This happened with a blind Chow named Gracie. By the time we met her she had already been through several shelters. Everyone who has had her loved Gracie, but no one has ever wanted Gracie because Gracie was a problem. Blind dogs often develop very reactive behaviors towards other animals because of fear, uncertainty and a lack of visual cues such as a tail wag or friendly posture. Gracie could not be housed around other dogs because she would lash out any time one came near.

She finally managed to get adopted by a lady in our area and we went immediately and provided training for her to help make sure the adoption was successful. The lady was entirely devoted to Gracie, but was frustrated because Gracie didn't seem to be reciprocating. She went through the motions but seemed disinterested. We had talked about possessiveness as fundamental to helping Gracie feel safe and although she understood it as a concept, but she wasn't quite getting it across.

One day she was walking Gracie and a stray dog charged them. She took a deep breath, stepped in front of Gracie and shouted at the stray, "this is MY dog, you BACK OFF!!!" and the stray stopped, turned and ran away. In that moment Gracie looked up at her (which is weird since she has no eyeballs. She'll look you right in the face, though) and she locked in. From then on Gracie bonded the way the lady had hoped for because someone had finally made her feel owned, which made her feel safe.

It's a difficult concept for many people, but in a dog's world feeling loved and feeling safe have little to do with each other. A dog can feel very loved, and not feel that someone else is caring for all their other needs besides affection. Almost every client we've ever had has provided love, affection, shelter, food and companionship to their dogs before they called us, and yet the dogs still had behavioral issues.

If love and affection were enough to fill all a dog's needs then everyone's dog would be well-behaved and we'd be out of a job. A dog also needs a feeling of safety and they need to have calm self-control taught every day. Most importantly they need to have a calm authority figure in their lives that will define their environment for them through possessiveness.

Personal Space

One of the most important things for you to feel possessive over is your own personal space. As a human, you have personal space. You have a little bubble you carry around with you that you expect every other human to respect. Your personal space may be larger or smaller depending on who it is, but everyone is supposed to respect your bubble. People are expected to be considerate, but dogs are allowed to crowd right up on us. They push, jump, crowd, sit on us, mouth at our hands, flop on our feet, and we generally tolerate it without giving it much attention.

When we are working with a group of dogs without any humans involved and we are getting a sense of the social order within the group, one of the primary things we look at is which dogs require the largest bubble of personal space. In other words, no one crowds the dogs at the top of the pack. The dogs at the bottom are being bumped, trampled, pushed, stepped on and being otherwise disrespected by the others. Dogs are inherently social, territorial animals. They understand the concept of personal space and they know it's rude to crowd. It is, however, the only way they have to ask what your personal space is so they can understand your place in the social order. What answer they receive is what is important to them.

From a dog's point of view, if you don't claim ownership of your own bubble of personal space, how can you possibly own the rest of the territory?

A dog should be required to respect your personal space (and your guests and each other's space as well) just as another human would be. If they crowd you, just stand up and back them away a few steps with a calm but disapproving attitude. You can invite them into your space any time you like for interaction, but when you are done they need to go back outside your bubble again. This is a vital concept to understand and it really takes some practice to get into the habit of doing it, but this is one of the most important things you can do to begin working through issues with dogs. Be diligent.

Understanding a Dog's Vocabulary

The need to ask about personal space is so basic for a dog that they have what you might call a vocabulary of gestures to discuss it. Dogs have to have some way to ask what the social order is, and a big part of how they do it is through a combination of gestures that add up to "can I crowd you or not?" There are three categories of gestures dogs make when they are discussing personal space, and anything you see the dogs do that looks like one or more of these gestures is them having a conversation about social order and a response is required.

The gestures are:

- "I'm in front"
- "I'm on top", and
- "I own the resources" (also known as "that's mine get away from it").

I'm In Front

"I'm in front" can be blatant gestures such as standing between a family member and a stranger or pulling at the end of the leash barking at strangers that walk by, but it can also be more subtle. For example, a dog laying across doorways or hallways is an "I'm in front" gesture. They are the first individual you have to interact with to enter that space. They are "in front" of the room. It's also things like a dog sitting in front of you with their back to you. They're guarding you like you're some kind of sheep. It is a gesture that communicates to others, "this is my human, and I'm in charge." They'll also do things like lean in front of you when you're standing with them on leash or lay in front of you while you're sitting to block others away from you.

I'm On Top

"I'm on top" are gestures such as jumping, pawing at you, stepping or sitting on you and other forms of crowding.

Have you ever seen one dog put its paws on another dog's back, or things like mounting behaviors? It's pretty clear when two dogs do these things that the dog on top is trying to assert themselves over the one on the bottom.

Paws on a person means essentially the same thing, "I'm as high up on you as I can be – I'm in charge of you." This is why jumping tends to be so insistent during re-unions. The dog is saying, "hey, you're home! Don't forget, I'm in charge."

"I'm on top" are also gestures like stepping on your feet, sitting on your feet, leaning into you, crowding your space and putting their head on your knee to demand attention. This may also come out in behaviors such as putting their paw up on your arm when you pet them. To be clear, they aren't petting you back. You're touching them on top – on the head or the shoulders, and they are saying, "no, I'm on top of you. You can pet me, but I'm in charge here." Think of it as trying to claim possession over your affection.

"I'm on top" is also the reason the best place for a dog to sleep is on the floor in an adult's bedroom. Dogs expect to sleep together so they need to be in the same room, but an authority doesn't share its actual sleeping space. Never isolate them away from you at night in another room or outside, but don't have them on the bed either. For a dog to be on top of you or your sleeping space during a primary pack activity – sleeping – is to tell the dog they have responsibility for the humans. Unfortunately, sleeping arrangements are not a point dogs generally can have unclear without it causing issues.

We do understand that sleeping arrangements are one of the most personal issues we involve ourselves in, and moving our dogs to the floor was the last piece of this approach we implemented in our own home. We enjoyed the warm fuzzy feelings we got from having them curled up with us at night. We also had some severe health issues at the time and it was very comforting to have the dogs close when we didn't feel well. We finally accepted that the dogs had to be moved to the floor when we set a boundary for one of our dogs and she looked us in the eye, jumped on the bed and pooped on it. It was the one weak spot in our structure and she took that as her opportunity to assert herself. After that it wasn't so hard to just move them to the floor and be done with it.

That's Mine, Get Away From It

"That's mine, get away from it" is all the possessiveness issues – food, toys, the dog beds and so on. Remember, in a natural dog pack only the leader owns anything. It's not the dog's bed, it's your bed the dog gets to lay on. Hoarding or guarding behaviors should not be allowed. If a dog tries to hoard things, go and take it and keep it. Don't put it away, and don't give it to another dog. Just walk around with it or sit with it (whatever it is) for awhile and let the dogs see you owning the resources. Remember, in that moment it's not just some slimy rope, it's a trophy of social order. After a few moments you can lose interest in it, drop it and walk away. If one dog pushes another off a bed, go and stand on it yourself with an attitude that fussing over space isn't allowed.

Miscommunication Makes Problems

It's important to understand that "I'm in front," "I'm on top," and "that's mine" are where miscommunication between dogs and humans usually begins. We misread and humanize these behaviors, and the misinterpretation of these gestures can cause problems in the family's relationship. What happens when a dog puts their head on a person's knee to demand attention? Usually they get pet. Have you ever seen what happens when a dog sticks its head over another dog's neck? A nasty fight can break out. It's serious to them who's on top, in front, and who owns the resources. The way to understand what these gestures mean is to watch how other dogs respond, because it's their vocabulary.

Here's a great example of how miscommunication happens. Imagine watching TV, and a dog sits down in front of you with their back to you and leans on you a little bit. What do people usually do? Most often they pet. They perceive the dog's behavior as being friendly, and it is, so they give affection. That's the tricky part for many people; none of this means the dog isn't being friendly. Remember, this isn't misbehavior, it's vocabulary. These gestures are part of play, part of affection, part of everything in a dog's world. "I'm in front," "I'm on top," and "that's mine" gestures are how dogs sort out social order without teeth and growling.

So yes, the dog is being friendly. However, you must always take the vocabulary into account. In this example, the dog has its back to you (I'm in front), it's leaning on you (I'm on top) and it's keeping everyone else away from you (that's mine, get away from it). The dog is giving all three gestures, and we reinforce that attitude by giving them affection. Why would a dog then be agreeable in other areas of its life? It's being told in its own vocabulary that being disrespectful is acceptable. It is being allowed to crowd personal space.

So what do you do about it? Remember, this is not misbehavior, it's communication. We don't discipline for these things – we participate in the conversation. The best way to think of this is that the dog is asking a question – "Can I crowd you?" We simply answer the question with a "No." Pick one of these gestures, and do it back. If a dog sits in front of you with their back to you, they are saying, "I'm in front of you, can I crowd?" Just stretch your legs over them. "No, I'm on top of you – I can crowd." If a dog puts a paw on your arm, put your hand on their paw. If you're walking them and they step on your feet, shoo them off, then lean in a little until they make room for you (don't step on their feet, you'll hurt them). It's "I'm in front," "I'm on top," and "that's mine" over and over again in different contexts.

The best thing to do is to have a sense of humor about it. This is also part of play so don't get upset about it, participate. Just make sure you actually pay attention to when the dog is discussing personal space and this sort of thing settles itself out easily. In each instance, when you are tired of playing set a boundary to end the conversation.

BRINGING IT TOGETHER

Hopefully it's become clear the value of paying attention to the little things each day that matter to a dog. Attention to these fundamental issues are necessary to fill its needs consistently. What's returned is a calm, focused and agreeable attitude that will make resolving problems much simpler. Take a moment now to think about the world of dog advice out there on the internet, in books and in classes everywhere: if the dog chases a cat shoot them with a squirt bottle (don't do that). If they bark at the window throw a can of pennies at them (don't do that, either). If they jump or bark shoot them in the face with Binaca (don't do any of these horrid things).

Chains, prongs, shock collars, newspapers, flyswatters - do any of these sorts of things make a dog calm? Do they make a dog more agreeable? Of course not, they generally make a dog a fearful, neurotic mess. No matter who tells you to do something, if it won't make your dog calmer and more agreeable than when you started it is NOT a good idea and you should not do it. Anything that does meet that basic standard is likely not too far off the mark. Remember that solutions aren't found in deterring negative behaviors but in establishing a pattern of calm responses throughout the day.

ADDRESSING SPECIFIC ISSUES

Specific issues can't be addressed without developing a good foundation of calm in the home, but once calm is in place there are often still habitual behaviors that need to be dealt with and rules that need to be taught. There are two concepts that are very helpful when teaching "house rules" to a dog:

- Identifying Moment of Intent
- Event Staging

Moment of Intent

Dogs are always communicating. They're broadcasting how they feel about themselves, everything around them, and if you're paying attention you can catch the moment they're making decisions. This is not the moment they act, it's the moment they're thinking about acting. It's what we call the "moment of intent" and it's the primary moment of learning for dogs.

A good example of the need to catch the moment of intent is working with a dog that gets into the trash. When first starting with a family for this issue the conversation typically goes something like this: "When we come in, before we've even seen the mess the dog is hid-

FROM SHELTER TO SERVICE DOG

ing under the table. He KNOWS he shouldn't have DONE THAT!"

In that situation, the only thing the dog knows for sure is at some time in the past trash was on the floor, humans came in and he got punished. The only lesson he learned is when there's trash on the floor, don't be around people. For the dog to make any sense out of being disciplined after-the-fact he would have to rationalize out, "OK, let's see. They get mad when the trash is ON the floor, so the next time I smell tuna in the trash can I'd better not knock over the can and lick the tuna because then the trash will be on the floor and I'll get in trouble again when they come home..."

That's logic. Dogs don't have logic. They have excellent problem-solving skills and they excel at identifying patterns in our behavior, but they do not rationalize the consequences of their actions. In that scenario the dog's only thought is, "Sniff, Sniff, Tuna! Yes or No?" All of a dog's decisions are basically Yes or No.

To influence a dog's decisions, you must be able to interact with the moment the decision is being made, which in this situation is the moment the dog sniffs the trash. When the dog asks, "Tuna! Yes or No?" and I answer, "No" consistently, before long the dog will get the point to leave the trash alone.

Event Staging

How do we catch the moment of intent consistently enough to teach house rules? This is achieved through what we call "event staging." We create opportunities for the negative behavior to surface so that we can correct and teach in a timely manner and on a schedule that is convenient for the family. For the scenario above, fill the trash with a bunch of stinky things and set it next to the TV while watching. Any time a dog sniffs at it, give a verbal correction. If necessary, get in between the trash and the dog and back them up a couple steps if they don't respond to the verbal cue.

With repetition, this process creates a new pattern of behavior by being consistent during the dog's moment of intent. Communication can then happen about preferred actions regarding the dog sniffing the trash. If the dog begins to take a wide berth around the trash can, give praise since that is the acceptable alternative to them sniffing at it. The pattern may need to be reinforced a few times once the trash is back where it belongs, but the dog should have a good understanding of the rules by then and should fall easily into pattern.

Bear in mind, the timing of when you correct is what communicates what you mean. If you correct when they are sniffing at the trash you're saying, "leave the trash alone."

If you correct after the mess is made but while the dog is still in it you are saying, "now that I'm here, give me that." That doesn't mean, don't get into it at all. It means, give it up when I come in. Correct when you catch them in the mess, but don't expect you've taught them not to do it again.

If correction comes after the mess is made and the dog has already left it the only thing being communicated is, "I don't like trash," but nothing at all about how the dog should interact with it. Correction after-the-fact is confusing for the dog and detrimental to training. No matter how frustrated you might feel, if you miss catching them in the act just remove the dog from the situation, clean up the mess and move on.

Event staging is the tool that defines a dog's world for them. Whether it's the trash, destruction of shoes and purses, house-training (discussed later), counter-surfing (stealing food from the counters and table) or any other rule that needs to be taught, the answer is usually the same. Figure out how to get the dog to do the behavior in a context that can be monitored so teaching can happen. In most cases, to correct the behavior either get directly between the object and the dog and back them directly away from the thing they shouldn't touch or use a leash to walk them through appropriate responses to triggers in their environment. If you are unsure about accomplishing that you should contact a competent trainer to help you.

The Road Map For Success

Assuming the system provided has been applied diligently, then within a few weeks of starting things should seem somewhat better. By this point, the dog should have calmed down significantly and have a lower default level of excitement. It should also have improved focus and attention and be more agreeable to structure in the home.

The only piece of the system that remains is to decide what rules should apply in the home and teaching them consistently. To that end, remember that dogs live in the present. They don't dwell on the past or future and they are always giving their full attention to what is currently going on around them. They do, however, follow patterns of behavior. They know how they will behave first thing in the morning, they know what they will do when you get out the food bowls, your shoes, the leash or when you begin any of the repetitive activities in their day.

These are habits the dog has picked up throughout its life that may need to be restructured. Bear in mind that they don't dwell on the reasons for their behavior – "Once there was this guy who always wore these boots who scared me and every time I see boots I think of that guy." They respond to associative triggers: man + boots = bad. Shoes + Mom = Crazy Excitement.

If you want to change a pattern of behavior in a dog, you have to be consistent with requiring the new behavior until the dog forgets the old one. That usually takes a minimum of 30-45 days. You have to continue requiring acceptable behavior after that, but by then it will be a habit for everyone and you won't have to think about it much any more.

Here's the trick, though. If you are inconsistent at any point during that time, start the clock over. Indeed. 30 – 45 days from THAT point you can have the behavior you want if you are consistent. It's one of the greatest pitfalls for families attempting to address behavioral issues. There can sometimes be more than one way to address an issue with a dog, but families don't do anything long enough for it to stick so they never get long-term improvements. They try an approach for a week or two and start to see some improvement, then slack off because now the dog is doing "better". Within a couple of weeks

THE ROAD MAP FOR SUCCESS

of no structure the dog's behaviors are back. After a few rounds of that the family throws up their hands and proclaim the dog untrainable.

This stems from not understanding how dogs learn. A dog is not just a bundle of conditioned responses that can be reprogrammed then left alone, and training a dog isn't like having a mechanic replace a broken part. A dog is an intelligent, communicative creature that learns best about its world through being given consistent, gentle guidance. For issues to stay resolved guidance has to continue for their entire lives.

To this end, we recommend you sit down with everyone in the family that interacts with the dog on a regular basis and make two lists. These lists comprise the rules and guidelines for the dog, and are your road map to success with this entire process.

The first list is easy – list all the negative behaviors. Here's a sample:

Negative Behaviors
    Jumping on people at the door
    Getting in the trash
    Chasing the cat
    Stealing food off the counters
    Tearing up shoes and pillows

Or it might look something like this:

Negative Behaviors
   Cowering away from strangers
   Jumping away from traffic
   Hiding under furniture
   Running from family members

Or this:

Negative Behaviors
   Barking at people that walk by the yard
   Barking and growling at guests at the door
   Growling at the children

Your list should contain any combination of these plus additions of behaviors that fit your situation. Be thorough. Our objective is for everyone in the home to be on the same page, literally and figuratively, with what behaviors will need to be addressed and what will not be allowed in any given situation.

The second list is the one that takes a bit more thought. This is a list of all the positive behaviors – specifically, what the acceptable alternative to each of those negative behaviors should be. Everything on this list should be phrased in positive terms, and should be specific. If a negative behavior is jumping on people the positive behavior isn't no jumping. That's still about jumping. That doesn't give the dog something to do instead. Also, being "friendly" or "well-behaved" are not descriptions of behavior. What does well-behaved look like? Guaranteed, no two people's idea of well-behaved are exactly the same. There should be specific criteria.

It may be that instead of jumping on guests the dog should bark a couple of times when the doorbell rings then back up 15 feet, sit down and wait for permission to interact. That would be an acceptable alternative to clobbering people at the door, and everyone can enforce it consistently.

Or, have whatever you want. That's the great thing about all this – you can have anything you want from your dog's behavior, but you have to know precisely what you want. If you don't know what good behavior is supposed to look like in very concrete terms, how is your dog supposed to figure it out?

Unfortunately, the relationship most people have with their dogs is that we discipline them for behaviors we don't like, we ignore them when their behavior is acceptable, and affection is random. Nothing in that pattern identifies what good behavior is supposed to be. Remember, it's not enough to tell a dog what they're doing wrong, the important part is to let them know when they get things right. This is how behavior is shaped over time. So, your lists might end up looking something like this:

Negative Behaviors	Positive Behaviors
• Jumping on people at the door	• Bark a couple of times, back up 15 feet, sit down and stay there
• Getting in the trash	• Stay 6 feet away from the trash can
• Chasing the cat	• Ignore the cat
• Stealing food off the counters	• Stay out of the kitchen unless invited
• Tearing up shoes and pillows	• Chewing on designated toys only
• Cowering away from strangers	• Sitting quietly or showing interest when strangers approach
• Jumping away from traffic	• Walking calmly near traffic

- Hiding under furniture
- Running from family members
- Barking at people that walk by the yard
- Barking and growling at guests at the door
- Growling at the children

- Laying by a family member's side
- Coming when called
- Moving away from the fence when people pass
- Sit calmly by a family member's side when company comes
- Disengaging when children get excited

Your lists will may include more than this, and the alternative behaviors should be specific to your needs. The goal is to get everyone in the house enforcing the same set of standards so come up with lists everyone can understand and live with. This often means a bit of compromise, but it's worth it to provide consistency for your dogs. These lists are key to success, so give them particular effort.

Wrapping Up Behavior

So that's how resolving behavioral issues works. We

have used this approach to deal with many hundreds of cases of rehabilitation, and have been successful in almost all of them. The only time this system is not effective is when the humans cannot or will not be diligent with applying it. Bear in mind, we are not describing a training method that is done to condition behaviors and then stopped, we're describing a life-style change. This is a fundamentally different way of living with dogs than most people have considered, and it must be kept up for the life of the dog if you want the behaviors you are correcting to stay resolved. Fortunately there are no permanent mistakes with dogs. If things slide you can always reset and put the system back in place, but it's better to not have to. Structure your day to fill your dog's needs then make a habit of it and the issues will stay settled.

ISSUES WORTH DISCUSSING

There are a number of specific issues and questions that arise repeatedly with dogs, and it is worth taking time to address each in detail. If a section does not apply to your situation feel free to skip ahead.

APPROPRIATE DISCIPLINE

What constitutes appropriate correction for dogs is at the heart of many of the divisions between professionals in the pet industry, and it can be a truly a contentious issue. Our experience has led us to a strong stance against physical correction and the use of pain as a motivator. As discussed earlier, in our opinion most of what passes for discipline with dogs is a bad ideas quirt bottles, chains, cans of pennies, shock collars, prong collars, rolled newspapers and so on are all detrimental to a healthy relationship and good control with a dog. So, what is appropriate discipline? When applied properly, there are two forms of correction that are effective in most situations: verbal correction and control of space (setting boundaries).

Verbal Correction

A verbal correction can be almost any noise you like that is short, sharp and unemotional. There are two noises we do not use for correction. First of all, we don't use a dog's name for correction. Their name is supposed to mean, come here and get love. It can't mean that and, you're in trouble as well. Dogs will associate only one meaning with a sound.

Second, we don't use "NO!" It takes too long to say, it sounds frustrated and the more you say it the more frustrated it becomes. If you like "NO!" then put a "pe" on the end – "Nope!" You can say that repetitively and not sound frustrated. We have a number of different corrective noises that we use. "Nope", "hep", "uh-uh", "hey", and so on. Whatever comes out of you naturally is generally fine. The noise itself has no power of its own; it's the timing of the noise that conveys meaning. In particular, a corrective noise should be timed to match a dog's moment of intent to perform an undesirable behavior. The noise catches their attention so they will look at you and see that you have a disapproving attitude. It's the attitude behind it that is the real correction – calm, focused and disapproving.

Setting Boundaries (control of space)

A dog is an inherently territorial creature. What that means is that every square inch of space matters to them, and a sense of losing space is a serious consequence. If a dog is exhibiting an undesirable behavior toward something or someone, give a verbal correction and perhaps a snap of the fingers the instant you notice. Immediately get in between them and whatever they were fussing at and back them away with a calm but very disapproving attitude. Step forward one step, then stand your ground. If they try to go around you, step forward another step to block their path and back them up again. Include a verbal correction each time a step forward must be taken. Repeat this pattern, backing the dog further and further from the initial point until they give up challenging and either sit down or lay down. Each step should feel like a statement with a period at the end – definitive.

This should not devolve into kneeing and pushing the dog. If the dog is uncooperative to the point of jumping or mouthing then keep a leash handy. The leash is only to have some way to keep them from touching you as you deal with their behavior. Slide the clip through the handle to make a lasso so the dog can be secured without needing to touch the collar and slip it over their head, but beyond that the boundary process should still be the focus of correction. Continue backing them up, one step at a time, until they give a little space and sit down. Boundaries are an incredibly useful tool, but only if performed in a calm way. Stay focused on the objective of the dog backing away from the thing they were originally fussing at and be methodical.

Every interaction with a dog is a conversation, and they need to be allowed to make a choice after each step forward that you take. Do they say, "no, I want to fuss at that (whatever it is)" by trying to go around you or do they say, "OK, I get it that I should leave that alone" by backing up and settling down? If they make the wrong choice back them up another step, adding a verbal correction, and wait for their choice again. This is the time for a calm, stubborn attitude from the human.

If you feel uncertain of your ability to handle your dog this way or feel that stepping between your dog and something they want would be unsafe for you then you DEFINITELY need to find a competent trainer that has experience working with challenging animals. Don't put yourself in a situation you can't control, and don't step up to get between them and something they are fussing at unless you are prepared to keep at it until they agree. If you set a rule and then give up halfway through, what you've done is teach them that if they are fussy enough they can get over on you. If you have a situation you're not sure you can manage, get a leash and use it to move the dog rather than backing them away. Walk them directly to the phone and call a trainer.

You may have noticed that we have not mentioned leash corrections or any sort of physical interactions as part of correction. When it comes to shaping behavior a leash is your best friend, but it is never for punishment or discipline. A leash is a tool for communication, guidance and teaching. It is not a tool for venting your frustration at the dog or for punishing them for poor behavior. A leash is used to teach them appropriate behavior, not to deter inappropriate behavior.

If you have a situation that cannot be controlled with either a verbal correction or a boundary, then put a leash on the dog before the behavior escalates so that you can institute healthy patterns and side-step the problems until new habits are established. For example, leashing a dog before beginning the feeding ritual can help prevent them from getting out of hand as the food comes out to make feeding more successful. If your dog can't be trusted to wander loose in the house without tearing things up, then keep them on leash and parked next to your side until they can be taught what is appropriate to chew on and what isn't.

Physical correction is never helpful and usually very detrimental. Understand that dogs learn directly from us. When working with dogs with reactive behaviors we often find a direct correlation between how the dog behaves and how the family disciplines. In particular, we find that if they smack the dog on the nose it will tend to bite at hands. If they smack the dog's rear it will tend to bite at people's legs. Physical correction simply teaches the dog that acting out at others is the way to deal with situations you don't like.

The Alpha-Roll, and Why You Shouldn't Do It

The "Alpha-Roll" is a technique that some people try as a means of making their dog be submissive when they don't approve of the dog's behavior. It involves laying the dog on their side and holding them at the neck. While it is true that dogs will sometimes roll another dog over and touch their neck with their mouth, it is important to understand that when dogs do this it is a ritualized behavior that does not involve force. The dog on the bottom is choosing to roll over to say, OK, we've got the order clear in response to the other dog's assertive energy. The dog on top is participating but not coercing.

This behavior is generally performed after social order is settled as more of a final gesture, not as a means to sort things out. When humans try it they generally grab the dog by the neck, body-slam them to the ground and then grip with force thinking they are dominating the dog. This is not a true perception of the situation. Intimidation is not teaching and fear is not cooperation. Social order is settled in the home in more gentle, gradual ways. Not to put too fine a point on it, but in our opinion very few people can do this technique correctly. You should leave this technique out of your toolkit. It won't serve you.

GLITTER AND DOG HAIR

It is a widely held misperception that children and dogs are an automatic fit. That is not really true. Sure, kids love dogs, but what about the dogs? Many children have a very erratic sort of energy about them that can be overwhelming for a dog, and the only way to guarantee safety for everyone is direct adult supervision. For example, when the kids are running around the yard screaming and bouncing on the trampoline is NOT the time for the dog to be left unattended around them. These situations create stress and nervousness in a dog and can very easily excite them to the point of acting out.

The dog also needs to always have the option to get away from the kids when they want to. The dog is NOT a babysitter or a toy or a way to distract the kids. No matter how tolerant a dog is, they all have limits to how much touching, hugging, kissing, pulling, chasing and yanking they can take. As discussed earlier, a dog has a need to live in an environment free from harassment, and young children generally aren't discerning enough to tell when a dog should have some space.

A good way to help define this is to teach children that when the dog is laying on a dog bed or in a crate that they must stay away and leave it alone. This creates a bubble of safety for the dog, since it has the option to go to the bed and have quiet time. The harder it is to regulate the children for any reason, the more a crate should be the choice. A physical barrier will help the dog feel more secure.

It is vital to understand that we never recommend that children be put into a position of trying to directly control a dog's behavior until they are teenagers. When a child has developed enough natural assertiveness to control a dog is individual to the child and only the parents can make that choice, but generally they begin being able to assert control sometime between 11 and 13 years old. We have worked with a 7 year old that was the most assertive individual in her home (she controlled both the dogs and the adults) and we've worked with 18 year olds that couldn't assert themselves at all. Be conservative about deciding when a child should begin to assist with direct control and rule-setting. It's always better to err on the side of caution.

The best thing a child can do if a dog does anything on your negative list is to walk away calmly and tell an adult. Bear in mind that by the time the adult gets there the moment of intent for the negative behavior has likely passed. Don't correct unless you can actually catch the behavior happening, but the child should disengage immediately regardless.

This does also mean that a child should never be considered a responsible sole caretaker for a dog. Buying a dog for the kids and expecting them to adequately care for it without direct, ongoing adult supervision is expecting too much and is setting the kids and the dog up for failure.

If you add a dog to your home you have to be prepared to care for it. If that's more responsibility than you have the time and energy for then consider getting a lower-maintenance pet such as cat, no matter how much your kids promise they'll do the work for a dog. Cats can be an excellent way to teach children to be responsible with pets without overwhelming them. Cats don't change their behavior if they receive affection all the time, eat when they feel like it, sleep on the bed and curl up in your lap for hours. As a bonus they put all their poop in one place. It's a level of maintenance a child can manage with very little supervision. Dogs simply take more work.

Dogs basically treat children as puppies. How do dogs discipline unruly puppies? Generally by growling or nipping at them. When an adult dog nips a puppy to correct them the family is often glad of it, since they are just as fed up with the puppy's behavior as the dog is.

When a dog nips a child for being inappropriate, however, it's an entirely different situation for the humans. From the dog's point of view it isn't doing anything different. It is still responding to unregulated behavior of the young. In our experience there aren't many unprovoked bites in a home. The family might not realize what happened to antagonize the dog, but that's not the same thing as a dog acting out for no reason.

All that being said, it is very important to understand how children should fit within the system we've presented. Generally, children can participate in obedience training, play, social exercise and work. They should ignore the dogs during reunions and can assist with feeding but shouldn't be left in charge. Children should never perform "I'm in front", "I'm on top," and "that's mine" gestures, even unintentionally. This means that kids should not lay on the dog, give them hugs or pull at their ears, tail or fur and the old adage that you should let sleeping dogs lie is particularly important for children. Letting a child get right in a dog's face or do things the dog might take as antagonistic actions is a REALLY bad idea.

A child simply isn't going to be able to identify when a dog is getting overwhelmed and back up before it acts out, and the kid is way too close for the parent to intervene if there is an issue. Children simply don't tune in to these sorts of things, so it is up to the parents to regulate interactions and teach good manners to the kids. Even if your dog is tolerant, other dogs your child interacts with may not be, and children need to learn appropriate behaviors in relation to all dogs.

Possibly at this point you are thinking something along the lines of, "aren't you being a bit over-reactive about all this? I grew up with dogs and my dogs never acted out at me for these sorts of things. I learned to walk by pulling myself up with the dog's fur and tail." It's true, there are many dogs that are very tolerant of children being inappropriate, but we have far too many clients with children with scarred faces, hands and arms because their dog was not one of those dogs. In our experience, it's a far better choice to be safe than sorry when it comes to kids and dogs, even if it means not allowing behaviors from the children that people may find endearing.

BARKING

Barking is one of the most common complaints dog owners (and neighbors) have about dogs. There are four primary reasons dogs bark, and each must be addressed differently. Dogs bark because of:

- Moments of perceived danger
- Unhealthy level of excitement
- Separation anxiety
- Reinforced habitual behavior

Barking in Relation to Perceived Dangers

Most often, dogs bark repetitively because of moments of perceived danger. They are upset because of some external trigger and no one has responded. Whether it's dogs on the other side of the wall in the back yard, strangers walking in front of the house, the FedEx guy, the mailman, hot air balloons or whatever, these are all moments of perceived danger and need to be dealt with as described earlier (Perceived Dangers pg. 64). For the behaviors to taper off consistency is required with getting up, getting in between, staying calm, feeling good and walking away. If the dog does not disengage, use a leash to walk them around until they calm down then take them inside or to a different room. Give no direct attention for the dogs at all during these moments. If you are reliable for them they will begin to desensitize to the triggers in their environment that are repetitive. If your dog is persistent about triggers in the yard they should not be left unattended outside.

Some people are concerned that if they teach healthier responses to perceived dangers their dog won't alert to threats around the home. Rest assured, a dog will reliably try to protect its family if there is a real threat in the environment. Responding to perceived dangers helps calm them about repetitive triggers but does not keep them from responding to unexpected noises or immediate challenges.

Here's an example of how this works: we used to live in a small apartment with three border collies (not a good choice, but we did it). The guy that lived directly across the sidewalk from us was disturbed. Pacing in front of his apartment in his underwear yelling at the voices in his head to leave him alone, laughing madly then crying-style disturbed. Understandably, every time he came out and started making noise our dogs would set off barking at him. We got up each time and did a moment of perceived danger, and they gradually settled down and stopped carrying on at him.

One day he came across the sidewalk to near our door. The dogs carried on as intensely as ever because we hadn't told them that it was alright for that guy to do anything else but pace in front of his door. They didn't want him any closer to our door (which was fine by us). Responding to moments of perceived danger doesn't teach a dog not to bark, it gives you a lever to get them to stop barking when you need them to.

Barking Due to an Unhealthy Level of Excitement

If your dog barks obsessively with a monotonous tone that carries on without a direct trigger, then your dog has an unhealthy level of excitement and persistent safety concerns about their environment. The barking is them asking to have their concerns addressed. Be diligent with applying the system presented in this book and get them some outlet for high-energy play or social exercise. In addition, the moment the fixated barking starts put them on leash and walk them around calmly until they let it go.

Dogs with these behaviors will always benefit from being kept on leash in the house next to a family member the majority of the time. In addition, get them enough exercise to be too tired to bark. This is one of the few situations where keeping them tired really is an important part of the formula. The structure must be in their day as well, but keeping them tired helps to build better habits.

Barking Due to Separation Anxiety

Dogs barking due to isolation is no different than them exhibiting other negative behaviors from isolation. It is addressed through diligence with reunions and addressing the dog's default level of excitement. Please read the section on Separation Anxiety for more information.

Barking (and Whining) Due to Reinforced Habitual Behavior

Dogs are smart creatures and they are very good at problem-solving certain kinds of puzzles. How to get attention, for example. Dogs will experiment with a wide range of behaviors to see what gets them direct engagement, and whatever works becomes a tool in their toolkit. Barking and whining are behaviors that can be easily reinforced, most often through eye contact (read affection). The dog barks or whines and someone looks at them. That becomes a behavior they will repeat any time they want attention or become stressed. Reinforced behavior of any sort will not taper off until the reinforcement stops completely. Certainly if there has been more direct reinforcement given (such as treats) it will take proportionately more diligence to taper the behaviors off.

To address these behaviors, keep the dog on leash by your side in the house. When barking or whining occurs, turn your back with an attitude that is calm but disapproving. When the whining stops, turn and make eye contact with a smile. If it starts again, turn your back. The same principle applies if the dog is in a crate. Even a small amount of attention will propagate the behavior so be diligent. Bear in mind that the dog should have some appropriate way to ask for attention. This is a good time to substitute the desired behavior as what does get your attention. As the behavior tapers off make sure to provide the dog with more constructive outlets for their pent up energy.

GUESTS IN THE HOME

A dog doesn't have to have a history of being reactive to have problems with strangers coming into the home. First of all, if you don't trust your dog to be reliably friendly then keep a leash next to the door and leash them or put them in a nose halter before you let a stranger in the house.

Answering the Door

Answering the door is a bit of a special case in the home. In the initial moments after the doorbell it's a moment of perceived danger. The dog knows someone is on the other side of the door. They will not settle down until the perceived danger is addressed. So, as with any other perceived danger, when the doorbell rings don't give the dogs any attention at all. Walk to the door, crack it just an inch or two and greet your guest. Ask them to hold on for a moment then close the door again. This friendly greeting defines for the dogs that you are accepting of the stranger and it lets the person know you'll be right with them so they don't ring the doorbell over and over again.

After you have addressed the stranger, then turn around and set a boundary far enough away from the door to get your guest in without being crowded. Ask your guest to ignore the dogs until you release them to greet. If you are unsure about your control of your dog's behavior then leash them before the guest is allowed in and keep them that way until they calm down completely.

If the dog is social, once the guest is in and settled and the dog is calm release them to greet. If they're not social then keep them on leash or in a crate in the same room. If you don't trust them then keeping them in a crate is best. It allows them to learn to be around strangers in the home without the risk of issues while also allowing you to be a good host and focus on your guests. Calmly correct them if they become fussy at the guest at any time, whether in a crate or on leash.

If guests are staying the night, bear in mind that the dog being alright with them the night before doesn't mean that they will automatically do well when encountering the guests the next morning coming out of a bedroom. Treat each new greeting separately and the dog will acclimate quickly.

HOUSE-TRAINING

House-training a dog is really very simple, but many people don't go about it correctly. First and most importantly, there is never, ever, ever, ever a place for disciplining a dog in relation to house-training. All that old-school advice you may have heard (rubbing their nose in the mess, swatting them with a newspaper, throwing them outside, bringing them back to the mess and scolding, etc.) is all a very bad idea. Don't do any of it.

If you can't interact with the moment of intent to eliminate you cannot teach them anything useful, so if you find a mess after it's made just clean it up and move on. Rough handling doesn't teach a dog what they should have done instead, it just makes them afraid to do their business in front of you. This makes them that much harder to house-train. They start hiding it behind the couch, in the closet, in your shoes... They do not have a choice about eliminating and should not be punished for it. They have to go somewhere, the family simply needs to adequately communicate "inside bad, outside good."

We were working with a shelter a few years ago that had a little Westie terrier dropped off because the family said he was vindictive about being house-trained and would mess in the closets, in the guest rooms, and everywhere they didn't want him to go. They said they had tried "everything" and had given up on ever being able to train him so they wanted to get rid of him.

We put him in a kennel with several other dogs, and later that day one of them messed on the floor. He saw the pile, then yelped and ran into the corner and stood shaking while hiding his head. It was obvious that he had been punished harshly when he made messes – to the point of being terrified – but the family had done such a poor job of teaching him that he had never even put it together that it was his mess that was the problem, let alone that it was the location of the mess that was actually the issue.

Fortunately, we were able to work through his responses with gentle handling. We then placed him with a different family that was willing to do things properly. Within a week or so he was going outside regularly and was able to have a new life in a better home. DO NOT discipline a dog for making a mess. Ever.

Here's the method we have developed for house-training that we have found to be extremely effective in most cases. It's another form of event staging.

- Get a really big bowl of water and mix in a can of

tuna, some beef broth, some wet dog food, or other enticement.

Make sure it is tuna packed in water, not tuna in oil. You will not improve house-training by giving your dog the runs.

- Put the dog on leash, bring them to the bowl and let them drink all they will.

The idea is that we're filling them up with all the liquid they can hold to create the need to pee. If the dog is really filled up, their full bladder will eventually overcome any hesitation they have to going in front of you.

- Once they have drank all they will, begin walking them through the house.

Keep them moving. Let them wander, but do not let them settle anywhere. Keep walking them past all the spots in the house they have gone previously and wait for the dog to make a choice about where to eliminate. Don't just take them out because you think they probably need to go. Wait for them to choose. If they don't seem interested in going, bring them back to the tuna-water some more until they are really full.

Make sure you take them through the entire house, especially areas they are not normally allowed. Dogs do

pg. 135

not identify inside as what's inside the walls. Inside is where they spend their time, and areas they don't normally go aren't part of the den. Areas like the formal dining room seem like great places to put the mess, since it's outside the areas they normally spend time with the family.

- When you see the dog preparing to release inside, give a gentle verbal correction so the dog will cinch up, take them quickly outside and stay with them until they relieve themselves, then praise them for doing it in the correct spot.

Be patient once you get them outside. They tightened up because you corrected them, so it may take a few minutes for them to relax and release. Don't stare at them. Keep them on leash but turn away so they don't feel nervous, then gently verbally praise as soon as they begin to go.

- If the dog leads you to the door, praise them at the door for making the appropriate choice, then praise them for eliminating outside as well.

- If you wish to teach your dog a potty command, then gently say the word or phrase you want as they begin to release, but not before.

Dogs have to associate the phrase with the action of releasing first, then you can gradually begin to say the phrase just before they release, and soon it will be a trigger for the action. The word or phrase can be anything you like, just make sure it's not something you would say around them in another context. "Go potty", "do your business", "go number one" or whatever are usually fine, since you aren't likely to say those things in conversation in the house (that might not be true if you have children). In our home, the potty command is "hurry up," since that's what we really want them to do (we house-trained our dogs in the middle of winter in Washington State).

It was made clear to us how important it is to pick an appropriate phrase when our mother got a little dog. The dog was 3 years old and had no house-training, so we got Mom started with crate-training and did event staging for her while she was at work. Out of habit we trained him to the "hurry up" command, and we thought we had things worked out in short order as he always went outside for us.

She kept complaining that he was messing on the stairs when she went to let him out in the morning, though. We eventually figured out that she was trying to get him to go down the stairs quickly to get him out. When she got to the landing she was telling him to "hurry up" and so he did as we taught him and did his business when he was told to. Turns out we had created a miscommunication problem due to choosing a phrase that wasn't appropriate for her.

- Bring them back in on leash and repeat the process.

Once you have really filled your dog up with liquid, they will probably need to eliminate every 10-15 minutes for two or three hours so set time aside for this project. Make sure you do this during the day so that they are able to completely empty themselves before bed time.

You will also get a very good idea of your dog's bladder strength from this exercise. If they are completely full but still only relieve themselves every half hour or so, they have pretty good bladder strength and should not have a problem holding it while in the house once they understand where to put the mess.

- Repeat the entire exercise once or twice a week until the messes stop.

We do not consider a dog fully house-trained until they are at least 30 days without a mess. Some dogs put this pattern together with only one round of event staging and some need consistent reinforcement. Just keep at it until you are sure the dog has gotten the point.

- Until a dog is fully trained they must be supervised at all times while in the house.

Keep them on leash in the house so that you can intervene during the moment of intent to eliminate. If they are able to wander off and make messes it will undermine the process. If you can't watch them directly for any reason, put them in a crate. Dogs have a natural aversion to messing where they sleep, so a crate will help them develop control.

Notes On House-Training

- No matter how small they are, do NOT pick a dog up and carry them outside.

The dog needs to perform the motor function of walking to the door or dog door and going outside. We've been in lots of homes where the little dog looks the owner in the eye, then pees on the floor right in front of them. The owner points at the dog and says in an exasperated tone, "LOOK! See? She's being vindictive!" No, she's not. Dogs are never vindictive (I can't say the same for cats).

What's going on is that when the family tried to house-train the dog, they picked her up and carried her out each time, teaching her that she is supposed to wait to be picked up. She looks at the person waiting for them to do their part by carrying her, then they don't so she just does her thing. The dog needs to go all the way through the action of walking to the door and going outside.

- If you have carpet or tile, the best thing to clean messes with is undiluted white vinegar (check for color-fastness).

Blot their mess with a towel, then pour on more than the dog did. Any kind of cleanser that comes in a spray will only clean the fibers of a carpet. The urine has soaked into the backing of the carpet and will attract the dog back to the spot even after it's been scrubbed. Vinegar poured on the spot will soak into the backing and break down the smell and is acidic enough that it won't mold the carpet. Do NOT use vinegar on wood floors or brick. You will not be happy with the results as it will strip the sealants. If you have wood or brick floors use a commercially available enzyme cleanser such as Nature's Miracle or other similar product. If you aren't sure where all the messes are in a carpeted room, you can get a carpet shampooer and fill the tank with vinegar and soak the whole floor. The vinegar smell dissipates as it dries.

- If a dog messes in their crate, it's often due to unsanitary handling by whoever had the dog's litter before 8 weeks old.

If young puppies are allowed to stay in their own mess and are not kept clean they can overcome their natural aversion to messing where they sleep. In this situation, make sure there is only enough room in the crate for them to lay down but not get off the pillow, and clean up any messes immediately and replace the bedding with something clean. With a little diligence the natural aversion usually re-asserts itself. Caveat: Some older dogs will urinate small amounts while sleeping, and will also often dribble urine while walking. This is incontinence and is a medical issue that should be discussed with your veterinarian who will likely prescribe a medication for it. It is not a behavioral issue. Incontinence can also be caused in female dogs of any age as a result of being spayed. It's not all that common, but it does happen. It's not malpractice, just a possible side-effect of the procedure.

- While a dog is being house-trained we recommend picking up the dog's water 2-3 hours before bed time so they have time to process all the urine out and can go to bed on an empty bladder.

Don't forget to put the water back in the morning.

- A dog's elimination system benefits from being manually stimulated.

It is often helpful for getting a dog to eliminate on a schedule to take them on a short walk right after feeding. The action of walking will help get things moving.

- What goes in on a regular schedule will come out on a regular schedule.

Try to feed at consistent times each day, and limit treats to once a day at a consistent time during the house-training process.

- Dogs, especially males, go through a period between 5 and 7 months old that we call developing marking bladder.

In essence, they begin to use the muscles that allow them to release urine in small bursts to be able to do marking of territory as adults. During this period they sometimes have very little control over those muscles. They get put out to do their business, they go, come right back in and piddle on the floor. They are not being bad. They went, but their bladder is still holding on to extra urine. During this stage, just leave them out a little longer and make sure they have the opportunity to go more than once and this behavior will stabilize within a few weeks in most cases.

- Knowing where to put the mess is not the same thing as being able to hold it.

If a dog has been trained to use a dog door their whole life they may never have had to develop any ability to wait to go. To teach bladder strength, use a crate at night or leash them to a piece of furniture so they can lay comfortably on a dog bed but not go anywhere. Their natural aversion to messing where they sleep will help them learn to hold it until an appropriate location is available. Start with about 2 hour blocks of time, then gradually extend it until they can hold it as long as is necessary for your environment.

For very young puppies, take them out every two hours around the clock. It's inconvenient, but the dog is an infant and needs to be treated accordingly. If you don't want to have to deal with getting up around the clock then don't get a puppy, get an older dog. By the time a dog is 3 – 4 months old you can begin with event staging and extending the puppy's bladder control.

HANDLING DRILLS

No matter how diligent you are at managing your dog and how others interact with it, situations will inevitably arise where it gets touched in ways that can be problematic. Whether it's going to the vet for a check up, being caught off guard by a child or being handled by unruly adults, at some point someone is going to touch your dog in a way that can create a potential issue. It's vital that dogs are being prepared for these sorts of things so that when the moment arises they are well-socialized and know not to act out. We accomplish this with handling drills.

Socializing a dog to touch is a simple enough concept – associate whatever you want to prepare them for with affection. For example, what sorts of things is your veterinarian going to have to do to examine your dog? They are going to have to open the mouth, look in the ears, check the eyes, handle the feet, palpitate the organs and lift the tail. We prepare our dogs for this eventuality by associating these things with gentle affection and love.

Start by gently tugging on the ears while petting the dog wherever they like affection best – scratch their chest, under their chin, or wherever. Begin socializing them to having their mouth opened by first lifting the lips, then gradually get a finger between the teeth and open the mouth for just a second. Finish with lots of love. At first you may only be able to lift the lips without the dog getting jumpy about it. Start with what you can do successfully and then gradually progress over time to the mouth fully open. Don't forget to add lots of affection for each step along the way. Prepare them for having their organs checked by gently pressing on their stomach in various places while petting them somewhere else. The same idea goes for lifting the tail. If you are uncomfortable handling your dog in this manner, contact a competent trainer to assist you.

Socializing your dog to the sort of handling required for an examination by the veterinarian is also important for accurate diagnosis. The only thing your vet has to go on initially to see if a dog is in pain is how they respond to being touched. If a dog isn't socialized to handling they will react poorly. The veterinarian will then have to order tests to find out if something is wrong. Not only is that more invasive for the dog but it costs more, too.

When we first began working with dogs, we fostered a little black dog named Cuddles that had been dropped at the shelter as a puppy and never adopted. Her whole life had been spent in a kennel and she had no socialization to touch. She also had an incontinence issue that we wanted to have checked so we took her to the veterinarian. They took her in the back room to examine her, and within a minute or so we heard a horrendous dog scream. They came back with dire predictions of a spinal injury. They had tried to roll her on her back and she had freaked out.

They wanted to do hundreds of dollars worth tests and send her to a specialist across the state to have an MRI – in other words, they wanted to spend a lot of money. That wasn't their motivation, but it would be the end result. We knew she was an active, bouncy sort of dog and we had not seen any sign of injury at home. We decided to take a couple of weeks and do handling drills with her, and when we brought her back she was fine. She simply hadn't ever been handled by a stranger that way and she had panicked. After the work we did with her they were able to take a urine sample from her and found she had a simple bladder infection that was treated with a round of antibiotics.

The other veterinarian-related issue your dog needs to be socialized to is the vet-tech grip. If your dog needs shots, a sensitive examination or other treatment your veterinarian will likely have a veterinary-technician hold them while they perform the procedure. This is a restraining hold that is for the safety of both the veterinarian and the vet-tech. They will wrap one arm around the dog's neck (as if hugging them) and wrap the other arm around their chest and hold them firmly. If your dog is not familiar with this they will tend to fight and struggle which makes it much harder for the procedure to get done. It also makes it much more likely that the vet-tech will get bit. If your dog bites the staff at your vet's office they may ask you not to come back. We have a number of clients that have to drive their dogs unreasonable distances for veterinary care because their dogs had habits of biting during exams.

Think now for a moment how a young child or unruly adult is likely to touch your dog. They will do things like hug the dog, pull the ears, fur and tail and put their face close to the dog's face. The same concepts apply for socializing to these things. Gently do each of these things while petting them in their favorite places.

If your dog is jumpy about having their feet handled, begin by brushing your hand down their legs as you pet. Slowly progress to lifting a foot, then to holding the paw, then to being able to handle the pads. It's important that you take the time to socialize your dog to having their feet handled. They need to have their nails trimmed periodically, you will have thorns and rocks to remove on occasion and you need to be able to handle their feet to wipe off mud and rock salt (rock salt can burn their skin if left between the paws). Just make it a gradual, steady process of socialization.

Socialization to touch is an easy enough process, but you have to do it every day as part of affection for it to do any good. When a two-year old is doing the "Frankenstein march" at your dog isn't the time to re-member, oh yeah, I was supposed to socialize my dog for this. It's way too late to do you any good at that point. These must be daily activities or they won't work when you need them. By associating all these sorts of things with affection, the dog will have a momentary hesitation when these things happen instead of simply lashing out from fear and uncertainty. This creates a window of op-portunity to intervene before things get out of hand.

FROM SHELTER TO SERVICE DOG

APPROPRIATE PLAY

Play is a vital part of a dog's life, and it is just as important to them as eating and sleeping. However, as with
most things, there is a preferred way for play to go. The
simple guidelines are these – play must always have
rules and should always be kept to a level of excitement
that is acceptable for everyone.

Rules for Play

- Play must always have rules but the rules can be very
simple.

What's required is that the dog perform a specific task
as part of the game, and there should be some point that
they must hold still for a moment. For example, fetch is a
game that has rules – actually it has five distinct steps: be
interested in the ball, chase it when thrown, pick it up,
bring it back and let it go. Fetch is a game that can be
very high-energy without losing control because it requires the dog to keep their brain engaged in the activity.
Playing tug-o-war with a rope or just wrestling with the
dog has no rules at all. The dog will escalate their energy
but they don't have to use their brain. It creates an unstable state of mind that's about physical contest with
others. That attitude rolls forward to other aspects of

their life.

- A dog's level of excitement during play must be acceptable for everyone.

Dogs are "all or nothing" in the way they learn and behave. If your brother-in-law likes to wrestle with your dog and be very physical, the dog will try to play that way with children, with older people and with anyone else they interact with. In addition, once those patterns are set it takes a whole lot of work to change them.

We worked with a family that had adopted a big adolescent dog named Stanley for Christmas, then had a family gathering the same week. The husband's brother (who is a huge guy) had thought it great fun to wrestle with the dog and encourage him to jump. The brother had only done this for a few days, but it set a pattern for how the dog should interact with others in his new home. The dog had then taken those behaviors and directed them at the wife who was a 5'2 petite woman. She was getting clobbered every time she walked in the house.

Stanley had also figured out that when she tried to correct him he could completely avoid her control by charging around the house and then knocking her over. We spent quite a long time working with them to reset those behaviors before she was able to achieve the level of control that she needed to manage him.

Dogs learn from their interactions with us. Don't ever do anything with a dog that you aren't willing to have them also do with others, including children and the elderly.

Appropriate Play is Structured Play

So what kinds of play are appropriate? Basically, anything that uses the dog's brain. Fetch is great, you can teach them a few basic agility skills by setting up some simple obstacles in the yard or get a hula-hoop and teaching the dog to jump through or crawl under it. You can teach them basic tracking skills (in particular, anything that lets a dog use their nose for a structured activity is immensely rewarding for them) or any number of other dog sports. There are endless resources available online or at your local library for dog games and activities. Pick something you think is fun, then do it.

The "Come When Called" Game

One of the best games you can teach a dog is to "come when called" (we call it the "Recall"). You might not have thought of "come when called" as a game, but if you want it to be a successful obedience skill it must also

FROM SHELTER TO SERVICE DOG

be really fun for the dog. If it's not a great game they won't care to do it if they have to choose between that and chasing rabbits, ducks, cars or little kids.

Above and beyond any other obedience skill, coming when called must work. If a dog won't "sit" or do a "down" the first time you ask, it's not a crisis. If a dog won't "come when called" the first time, that can be a crisis. To make the skill completely reliable we make it a game.

In our approach we teach this game in three steps, and we teach it in reverse. Notice that there is no mention of using treats during this process. For our purposes, we do not advocate using treats for training. We practice positive reinforcement, but the most powerful motivator you have is your sincere praise and affection.

Step One – The Finish

Before worrying about whether a dog will "come" from far away, we have to teach the concept of the game and we have to let them know how it's supposed to end. A dog that runs at you then takes a big lap around you and takes off again is not performing a successful skill. The point of the "Recall" is to get your hands on the dog. In practice, if your dog is loose and you call them you probably want to leash them. The dog needs to know to come directly to you, wait for you to touch their collar and then get lots of praise.

Here's how we teach it: Put the dog on a six foot leash and have them sit and stay (if they can't do that then you now have two more games to teach). Step to the end of the leash, then kneel down with your arms wide and call them with a fun, happy tone (no Drill-Sergeant voices) and as they come to you wrap them up in your arms and touch their collar as you share affection.

Make sure the praise is really sincere, but not fast and exciting. Fast scratching, giving the dog a noogie or banging on their sides are not effective forms of affection for training. Those sorts of things make a dog excited without providing a sense of reward. Keep your praise sincere and heart-felt but not fussy and excitable. Do this step in lots of different environments until the dog's response is 100% reliable and enthusiastic at a six foot distance.

Step Two – Adding Play

The second step turns this activity into a game. Dogs love playing chase. What we do is use a dog's natural inclination to chase things that move to our advantage. The technical term is creating a "conditioned fixation response." In other words, when I call a dog to me I don't want them to wander in my direction and stop along the way to sniff the grass and chase the bunnies, I want them to lock in on me and come to me with enthusiasm. This is created by adding motion and a little bit of chase activity to the "Recall".

Begin as in step one with the dog in a sit-stay on a six foot leash. When you call them and they start to move towards you, begin to move backwards. If they get distracted while coming to you then change directions and call them again to get them to reengage. When you see a little bit of bouncy "hey this is fun!" sort of reaction in the dog then stop and finish as in step one. Make sure you pay attention to what's behind you as you move around. Don't move faster than you can manage safely, and don't fall and hurt yourself. Practice this step until the dog's enthusiasm is immediate and reliable.

Step Three – Adding Distance

Only when both of the earlier steps are completely reliable should you begin to add distance. Start by clipping an extra leash onto the handle of your six foot leash to double the length. You can also get a long training lead (they usually come in 25' or 30' lengths), or you can use a long rope or a retractable leash. Do not try moving to longer distances without some sort of lead, though. You must have some way to reinforce the pattern that the dog must always come when called. You need a way to get them moving a little if they don't come on their own.

When training obedience skills of any kind, always build on success and don't get ahead of the dog's ability to respond accurately. At first it may be that you can get nine feet away instead of six, but past that the dog doesn't focus on the task. Start with what you can do successfully then gradually add more distance as the dog progresses. If the dog loses their focus during the activity, default back to Step Two and move backwards while calling them to you to turn it back into the chase game. They will get better and better with practice.

Appropriate Play With Other Dogs

Many people think of social behavior as being able to play with other dogs. That is certainly part of it, but if the focus is always on play then the most important element of social behavior is being missed – being able to leave other dogs alone. Have you ever known anyone with one of those awesome dogs that can walk easily with them in public and that lays by their side looking calm regardless of what goes on around them? It doesn't seem awesome because it's being friendly at everyone, but because it's minding its own business. That is a dog that has been taught to disengage and ignore others.

For a dog to be truly social they need to be able to be in the same environment with other dogs and not fixate. Make sure that during all play sessions with other dogs there is a point where your dog is required to lay quietly by your side and ignore the others. We prefer to start every interaction with the dogs walking around on leash until they can ignore each other, then letting them play as reward. Afterward, we finish with calm on leash again to make sure the high-energy interactions have a specific healthy context. Teaching appropriate play behavior with other dogs requires a lot of diligence, but it is important for having a social dog that is able to be well-behaved and responsive around other animals.

Most of what passes for dog play in peoples' homes or at the dog park is entirely unhelpful for creating stable behavior. Biting at each other's necks, rolling another dog over and standing over them, climbing on top of each other, growling, snapping, uncontrolled rough-housing – it's all inappropriate. This stands in contrast to many peoples' perceptions. "The dogs look like they are having such a great time. What's wrong with it?" What's wrong is that it's just an attitude shift away from a nasty fight. The level of excitement is extremely high, and if it were attached to less social behavior it would be a huge problem.

The level of excitement that is part of that sort of play becomes a very different thing when it's at the end of a leash pointed at a strange dog or up against a fence at dogs outside the yard. Letting a dog play that way doesn't teach manners or self-control and it encourages a dog to be fixated and pushy towards others. Even if dogs in a home can have rough-and-tumble play without escalating, aiming that sort of excitement at a dog that's reactive or insecure would become serious very quickly.

Here's the pattern this kind of play tends to create – when a dog is allowed to interact with other animals with uncontrolled behavior, they bring an escalated level of excitement to the play. Each time it gets a little more intense, until eventually the moment they see another dog they tense up, fixate and move forward. This can escalate quickly to the point of a fight.

So what is appropriate play? The best form of play between dogs is chase. Dogs that play well will catch each other's eye, strike a play pose (with the rump up and the head down), pause for a moment then burst into running around and chasing each other. They'll do that for a bit, then stop and repeat the pattern. They may get close to each other but they don't really touch. Once they have tired themselves out they will stop and lay together with big smiles on their faces. It's alright for them to bump into each other a little as long as there isn't any biting, growling or climbing on top of each other.

The best way to think of your role supervising dogs playing is that you are the referee. A referee doesn't stop the game, they call the fouls. The moment you see a behavior that you don't want, barge in the middle with a verbal correction and break it up, then let play resume. If you are consistent with the behaviors you correct, the dogs will begin to self-regulate and develop forms of play that are acceptable.

A Word About Dog Parks and Doggie Day Care

Dog parks are a sort of "no-man's land" that require common sense and a discerning eye. There is no lifeguard to enforce standards of behavior or safety. Other people's idea of acceptable behavior may not be the same as yours, and people tend to get upset when you correct their dog for being pushy or forward with yours. We prefer that our clients avoid them altogether, but if you are going to take your dog to a dog park then go during the off-hours when there aren't excessive numbers of dogs there, and have a very critical eye about the behaviors you see going on before you enter.

Dogs learn from each other as well as us. If you see behaviors going on in the park that you don't want your dog to emulate, then that's a good day to go do something else and skip the dog park altogether. Never take them inside until they are calm and can walk around the outside of the park ignoring the other dogs. If you can't make that happen then your dog isn't ready to be loose with other dogs and needs more work on calming down around others.

Regardless of what others do, always keep your dog on leash all the way from the car to the gate. Letting a dog run loose outside a dog park is inconsiderate to others and unsafe for your dog.

We also do not recommend doggie day care for dogs. In most day care facilities the dogs are put in groups and allowed to rough-house. The staff will generally not intervene until the teeth come out. Long before that point your dog has learned all sorts of negative behaviors that will spill over into how they interact with others in your home and in public.

We have had clients that began with us when they got young puppies to establish good control and socialization. They got good responses from their dogs while young, then as adolescence came on they began sending the dog to day care to let them burn off extra energy. The dogs began to play more and more intensely with others to the point that they became reactive to other dogs. It's never a good idea to allow your dog to interact with others without your direct supervision.

Appropriate Toys

Choosing appropriate toys for dogs is straightforward, but there are some common mistakes that can create issues. Addressing these few points can help ensure play isn't unintentionally setting a dog up for problems.

- Do not provide toys that even vaguely resemble things you don't want your dog to chew up.

Rubber TV remotes, fake stuffed shoes, rubber newspapers, or anything else that represents something you wouldn't actually want torn to pieces are not helpful. If you have children in the house, do not buy the dog stuffed toys at all. They can't easily tell the difference between a stuffed dog toy and a stuffed baby toy, so help them out. Make sure their toys are things like rubber bones, Nylabones, rope toys or other things that have nothing to do with resembling kids' toys.

Do not give your dog your old shoes to play with. They can't discern your old loafers from your $300 Armani dress shoes, nor is it appropriate for them to chew on things that smell like you.

- As stated in the Feeding Ritual section, DO NOT put food in toys, ever.

Do you need me to harp on it again? Never, ever, ever, ever....

- Do not provide toys that resemble small animals, or toys with squeakers.

The vast majority of dog toys have squeakers in them, but they are not helpful for creating a calm state of mind. Squeakers sound like small animals and can trigger the genetics that accompany predatory instincts.

Have you ever noticed how dogs tend to play with toys with squeakers? They chew, chew, chew then pick it up and whip it side to side. That's how a dog would kill an animal such as a mouse, rabbit or cat. It's a morbid thought, but a dog is a domesticated predator and it's unhealthy to stimulate a prey drive in them. Poke holes in the squeakers so they don't make noise, but don't give toys that look like animals of any kind.

- We strongly recommend against giving a dog any kind of real bones.

Real bones are prone to splintering and breaking off in chunks that can cause obstructions in the dog's intestines. We have many clients that have given their dogs real bones for years and not had a problem with it, and we have just as many that have had to pay for the $1000+ obstruction surgery. Best case scenario once a dog gets an obstruction is the veterinarian will give the dog powerful laxatives that will explode at unexpected times in the house or yard... After that comes surgery. It's true that uncooked real bones aren't as likely to splinter, but dogs can be susceptible to food-borne illness and uncooked bone lying on the floor is unsanitary. A good natural product for them to chew is antler. Antler is all mineral, won't splinter and lasts a long time.

- Rawhides are not toys, they are food and should be handled accordingly.

Obviously you wouldn't substitute a rawhide for a dog's meal, but to the dog it is a consumable and it should be regulated just like feeding. Give rawhides that are appropriately sized for them to finish within 10-20 minutes and park the dog in one place to eat it. If they try to walk away pick it up just as you would a bowl of food. You can leash the dog in place until they finish if you need additional control. Give appropriate sized pieces that they can finish in one sitting so that you do not have to take the rawhide away from them unless they try to walk away with it. Don't let a dog hoard them or hide them in the yard.

Some people take issue with rawhides and consider them a choking hazard. It's possible that some dogs might chew them so fast that they swallowed large chunks, but that doesn't generally occur in a dog that is otherwise calm. Give pieces such as flat chips, knotted bone-shaped pieces, or rolled hide with filling that are appropriate for a dog's size to avoid issues. Since you should not leave a dog unattended with a food product you should be able to monitor whether any problems arise and deal with them in a timely manner. It is true that giving a dog too much at once will cause intestinal upset, so be moderate.

Toys That Work

To make things simple for your dog you should stick to toys such as tennis balls, ropes, rubber bones and other toys that are similar in concept. Our dogs have a special fondness for the "Tire-Biter" toys, which are small rubber tires with a knotted rope strung through them. They're heavy and incredibly durable and the dogs love to whip them around in circles and play fetch with them.

A few of our clients like to give their dogs empty soda bottles to play with. The dogs love the crinkling sound, and it doesn't generally cause problems. We did decide that wasn't the best choice for our house when one of our dogs grabbed hold of a full soda bottle, threw it around the room, then punctured it with a good bite. I admit it was hilarious, right up to the point of cleaning up the mess.

A Special Note About Teething

Dogs start off with puppy teeth that they begin to lose somewhere between 3 and 5 months old as they grow in their adult teeth. Around this time you may notice your puppy beginning to chew on harder things such as wood (often chair and table legs, unfortunately) or metal. They are cutting new teeth. You can redirect teething to appropriate objects, but they have to chew something so you can't just correct them for it. They do make teething toys for dogs, but you may also find they like things like ice cubes or knotted ropes soaked in water then frozen. The cold helps numb the gums and will help with teething pain. They should also be directed to hard rubber toys that can be sanitized on a regular basis. When teething, a dog has open sores in their mouth as the teeth cut and cloth toys laying on the floor will harbor bacteria that can cause infections.

If you catch them starting to chew something they shouldn't give a verbal correction, feel possessive of whatever they were chewing and substitute something appropriate. Make sure you substitute something that was already available, such as a toy that was on the floor or in an accessible toy basket. Do not go get a treat or toy that they didn't have access to already, or the dog may learn to chew things just to get the special treat. When they give their attention to whatever you gave as a substitute, make sure to gently praise them for chewing on the appropriate toy to encourage good behavior.

FROM SHELTER TO SERVICE DOG

STAGES OF DEVELOPMENT IN PUPPIES

Raising a puppy is a huge amount of work. Make no mistake about it – puppies make me appreciate adult dogs. It takes endless maintenance and patience to raise them properly. No matter how cute they are they have to be taught manners, house-training, obedience, socialization to all sorts of things (strangers, other animals, traffic, new environments, etc.) and they have the attention span of a gnat.

Understand, though, the patterns that are set in a dog's life from birth to 6 months set the tone for everything that comes after, and if you wish to have a social, well-behaved adult dog then there is no room for complacency or being too busy to tend their needs and direct their development. You get one chance to do things right. After that you are stepping into the realm of behavioral rehabilitation to teach them appropriate behaviors. Problems can be fixed, it's just more work to go back and correct mistakes than to raise them correctly from the beginning.

For puppies and adolescents, it is necessary to substitute social exercise for maturity. You cannot give them too much exercise and interaction, and it is far more ef-

FROM SHELTER TO SERVICE DOG

fective to give exercise and play in several smaller doses throughout the day than to do an hour or two of concentrated exercise once. No matter how much you exercise them, as soon as they nap they will be ready for more, so break it up throughout the day.

There are a number of developmental stages a puppy goes through, and each has to be handled appropriately to end up with a well-balanced adult dog. These are the phases that are most pertinent for socializing and handling a puppy appropriately. Some of these developmental periods overlap, as some dogs enter phases at different times. There are more developmental stages than we list, but we choose to focus on what we find most pertinent for socialization.

Birth to 28 Days Old

During this initial period, puppies are focused mainly on eating and sleeping, and personality begins to express itself during this time. Eyes and ears open during this period and the puppy begins to interact with its environment and litter-mates.

4 to 12 Weeks Old – Initial Socialization / Primary Socialization Period

During this period puppies set the patterns for how they

will socialize with other animals through interactions with their litter-mates and older dogs. This is an absolutely critical period for dogs, and a puppy should NEVER be removed from its litter before 8 – 9 weeks old. At this point, a couple of weeks make a huge difference, and we find that the majority of the reactive, anti-social dogs we work with were pulled from their litter before that time.

When a puppy is removed from its litter too early, they do not develop good foundations for how to greet other dogs or have appropriate play, and they develop patterns of reactive behavior that take a lot of work to overcome later. Reputable breeders understand this concept, and will often keep a litter together until as late as 12 weeks old, but will not let them go before 8 weeks.

This period is also when a puppy looks to establish its first bonds outside its litter. If possible, go to where the litter is kept and spend time with the puppy to begin to create the bond you want with them, but only remove them from their litter to socialize for very short periods of time. Once they are placed with your family continue exposing them to as wide a range of people and animals as their health allows for. Puppies that have not had all their shots should only be exposed to dogs that are known to be healthy.

During this period, puppies create the patterns of response to new experiences that will become long-term behaviors. It is important that the puppy receive many positive, new experiences during this time. This is the time to introduce children, cats, strangers of various ages and other things the puppy needs to be socialized to.

If a puppy has a fear reaction to something, do not try to comfort them or pick them up (refer to the sections on Moments of Perceived Danger and Affection). They need to learn to adjust to uncertain situations at their own pace. Let them settle down, then if possible bring them back to the trigger again and let them explore it, whatever it is. If it's an object, touch it first then tap it and call them over and let them figure it out (many dogs have particular issues with things like statues and mannequins – just treat it all the same, regardless of what the object is).

If it's a person the puppy has a fear reaction to, have them turn their back and let the puppy approach and smell until they are comfortable. Once the puppy settles down the person can pet gently if the puppy accepts it. If there is still a negative reaction, then focus on the puppy giving attention to the owner instead of the stranger until they calm down.

A puppy needs to learn to socialize and greet strange

dogs, but to not get overwhelmed. If the other dogs rush up and plow them over or knock them down it can make the puppy afraid of initial greetings with dogs, so make sure everyone is playing nice. If you don't trust the other dog to be well-mannered don't let your puppy interact at all. If the other dogs don't seem inclined to show decent manners, do not pick the puppy up if you can avoid it (that's an "I'm on top" gesture from the puppy to the older dogs – it typically doesn't go very well). Just put them in another area and keep them separate. Dogs learn from each other, especially when young, and you don't want your puppy learning to be overbearing from a poorly-mannered dog.

12 to 30 Weeks Old – Juvenile / Secondary Socialization Period

This is the appropriate time to begin developing simple control exercises and to introduce early obedience training. It is somewhere around 16 weeks old that a puppy begins to be able to focus and can start to learn the way an adult dog learns. They have no maturity and not much attention span to go with their learning capacity, but they can begin to perform structured activities and exhibit focus and self-control in small doses.

During this time the initial patterns created during

their primary socialization period are reinforced. Make sure they are continuing to be exposed to typical fear triggers in and outside the home (the vacuum, traffic, car rides, etc.) in a positive way. In particular, there needs to be a strong emphasis on properly socializing with lots of different dogs during this time. By 16 weeks old their shots are usually complete, so get busy and socialize them. Read the sections on Appropriate Play With Other Dogs for information.

6 Months to 2 Years Old – Adolescence

During this period the dog is a teenager. Dog teenagers have all the same basic issues as human teenagers – they are headstrong, independent, higher energy and they will only listen when they have to. Essentially, they become a little hard to live with. Dogs have an escalation of their energy and focus on their environment around 6 months that continues until about 9 months old. Between 9 and 14 months is usually the worst a dog's behavior will ever be, and they require particular diligence during this time.

Animal shelters are full of adolescent dogs for just this reason. The original family didn't train or socialize the puppy when young (while it's still relatively easy), then the teenager behaviors come out. The dog is now a problem and isn't cute and fluffy any more so they dump it off. Doing the right work early will keep this period manageable until they grow out of it. If the fussy adolescent behaviors aren't regulated, however, they will carry forward and become adult behaviors.

What To Do With A Puppy

What all this information boils down to is socialize, socialize, socialize. There is no such thing as too much exposure to new things during puppy-hood and adolescence, but there is such a thing as not enough. It's a lot of work, and having to manage all this is not what people have in mind when the kids pick the puppy out of the cardboard box. It is, nonetheless, the adult's responsibility to make sure these things happen. Making it a low priority, never taking the puppy out of your home or leaving it up to the kids to manage is a sure-fire way to end up with a dog that is reactive to others and who displays a broad range of possible behavioral issues. Do the work up front and the tone will be set for having a well-adjusted dog that is social for a lifetime.

AGGRESSION AND REACTIVITY

Aggression is a loaded term in the dog world, and we use it very sparingly. There are three characteristics that define what we would see as real aggression:

- The behavior is immediate and without provocation. The moment they see a target, they attack and keep attacking.

- The behavior is intense at a level that is completely indiscriminate of who gets in the way, and has an intent to cause harm.

-The behavior is ongoing, meaning the dog has to be restrained to snap them out of it. They do not disengage on their own.

This simply doesn't define the behaviors of most dogs, even if they are exhibiting teeth and growling. If you feel your dog does fit this description, then while the information presented here will be helpful, it will not address all of your dogs needs. Competent direct supervision from an experienced trainer is generally necessary to work with aggression.

Most dogs that exhibit growling and biting behaviors we define as reactive. The main distinction is that reactive behavior is motivated by fear, and is entirely based in making threats go away – not a desire to harm others. That's not to say that if someone gets bit by your dog they will make the same distinction, but it matters for addressing the issues. When people think of their dog as aggressive they tend to take a heavy hand to controlling them. A dog that is reactive from fear needs to be made to feel safe and an overbearing approach won't get them there.

Reactive behavior is addressed in the long-term by addressing the dog's safety concerns and level of excitement, but along the way reactive behavior can be very challenging to manage. We have nothing but respect for families that stand by their dog and help them rather than getting rid of them or putting them down, and our experience is that any dog can be helped. One of our primary goals is to support those that don't won't give up no matter what.

We do make a point with our clients, however, to make sure they understand how challenging working a dog through reactive behavior can be. It can be done and we always support people for doing it, but it is not a process that is practical in every home. The family needs to make good choices for the safety and health of both the dog and the humans. The information listed here is meant to address the safety concerns associated with severe issues and is meant to provide some level of guidance, not to deter people from choosing to work with their dogs. Take the advice that is appropriate for your situation, and don't hesitate to seek professional assistance.

OK, The Warnings

Reactive behavior in dogs is a very serious and potentially disastrous issue, and we have seen people do all kinds of crazy, inhumane things trying to stop it. The reality is that dealing with reactive behavior in dogs is a challenging task and cannot really be adequately covered in a book of any size. Handling a reactive dog requires developing the ability to read very subtle cues in a dog's posture and attitude that signal an impending outburst as well as addressing the motivating fear underlying reactive behavior.

Through our career we've acquired more bite scars than we can count. Getting bit is a very real, present danger when dealing with reactive animals, even if the dog knows and loves you. Once a dog's level of excitement rises above a 7 and their behavior becomes unregulated they can simply no longer differentiate who they are snapping at.

The particular type of reactive behavior will determine the level of assistance you need (a dog that acts out on the walk toward dogs behind a fence is a whole different matter to handle from a dog that growls and snaps at family members) but you should always have at least some level of assistance from a competent trainer. Don't try to deal with reactivity completely on your own unless you have no other choice.

If you think you can handle it on your own or can't find a competent trainer in your area that is willing to work with a reactive dog, at least don't try to address reactive behavior without another person there to assist if things go badly. If you choose to try to address reactive behavior yourself, you are taking responsibility for how it goes and you need to be mindful of your own safety and the safety of others at all times. It goes without saying (but it will get said anyway) that the advice presented here is to help you understand the problems and have some context for approaching them. You must apply common sense and good judgment in all cases. As stated at the beginning of the book, you are responsible for your dog and its actions.

How Reactivity Works

All that having been said, there are some things to understand about reactive behaviors that will greatly improve your chances of finding the right help and addressing the issues successfully. When discussing reactive behavior, people often break the behaviors down into many isolated categories: food aggression, toy aggression, possessiveness of the owner, fence fighting, bed possessiveness etc., as if these were unrelated issues. When addressing reactive behavior, there are only three categories that affect how the family should respond – reactive behaviors toward external triggers, In-fighting, and reactive behaviors toward the humans in the family. Before we get into all that, there are a few concepts to cover that apply in all situations.

Fear

In all the hundreds of cases of reactive behavior we have worked with we have met only one dog that we felt truly had an intent to cause harm for no other reason than just to do it. That particular dog was badly in-bred and was severely short-circuited. He'd see you, get a look in his eye that said, "I don't like your kind, boy" then attack with no other consideration except to do you in. His behavior was due to irresponsible breeding and poor socialization. Every other case of reactive behavior we have worked with was motivated in one way or another by fear and a lack of a sense of safety and regulation in the dog's environment.

When a dog is acting out from fear, it is usually because they lack the sorts of structure discussed earlier in this book, and in particular they don't feel that anyone else is solving their problems (their moments of perceived danger) or feeling possessive of them. Be diligent with the entire system we've presented in this book, and in particular pay attention to moments of perceived danger. You have to make them feel safe if you want the behaviors to taper off.

Eye Contact

Reactive behaviors are often triggered by eye contact. Staring is conflict, and from the moment dogs lock eyes on each other or a stranger they escalate. That escalation happens in fractions of a second. The key to keeping a dog from acting out is to not let them look at other people or dogs during moments of tension. There are several ways to accomplish the task, but regulating what a dog looks at is a fundamental aspect in controlling reactive responses. It is one of the reasons we have a preference for nose halters, as it allows the dog's line of sight to be redirected easily. This issue can also be moderated by switching your dog to the opposite side of you from another dog when walking, turning them away, or blocking their sight in some other way until the trigger has passed. If they are allowed to stare, however, they will escalate. Don't wait to see if the dog is going to act out, just don't let them look at all.

Once a dog can disengage from a trigger and calm down when asked, then the handler can begin to ask for eye contact as a redirection from the trigger rather than directly controlling. When the dog looks up, make sure the praise is sincere and immediate to reinforce the pattern of looking at you when they are upset. With practice and diligence they can be gradually allowed more freedoms to look around as they learn to not get excited about it.

The Need For Structure

Here's the story of our dog Tug and why structure is so important in managing reactive behavior. Tug is a Rottweiler / American Bulldog cross. He's a beefy, barrel-chested 90 lb. boy with a Rotti snout and a pronounced under-bite. He was 5 years old when we got him, and he had been through at least eight different homes, rescues and shelters before we took him in.

We had done training with him previously while he was still with another family, due to a habit he had of biting people when he felt threatened. We had explained how to deal with the issues, but by the time we got there the family was already afraid of him and wasn't willing to do the work that was necessary to help him balance his behavior.

We made arrangements to have him taken by a rescue, and had him put into foster care with a family that had known him previous to being placed with his last family. Things were much better for him there, of course. They loved him and thought he was endearing, if fussy – we got emails from them saying things like, "Tug just grabbed my shoes and ran outside" or "Tug just dragged the comforter off my bed and out the dog door."

Tug would do things like walk up to someone with a big smile on his face, lean into their legs and push them over. He'd drag pillows and blankets into the yard, but was otherwise manageable. We explained that even this much was allowing him to develop an attitude that would lead to problems, and although they listened to us they also had several other dogs in foster and simply didn't have the time to give him the focus he required.

This continued for a few months, then the inevitable happened. One night, some family were staying over and walked into the house unannounced. By then Tug had it clearly in his mind that he was in charge and he was having none of it. He had the guests pinned in a corner, barking like crazy and spinning circles before the foster mom could get in between and back him off.

They managed to control the situation without anyone getting hurt, fortunately, but were understandably rattled by the whole thing. It became clear that we needed to take him if he was going to be managed successfully. We brought him into our home, began instituting good daily routines and established clear parameters for him. Once he was with our group, his whole demeanor changed. Through providing daily structure and not allowing him to do "I'm in front", "I'm on top", and "That's mine" gestures to us he settled down quickly and was able to let his stress and anxiety go.

Underneath all the fuss we found a loving, gentle, sweet boy that was simply easily overwhelmed. Once his needs were met he was able to relax, and now he spends most of his time just laying around in the sun or curled up next to the wood-burning stove in the evenings. He's not overly pushy and he is responsive to control and direction. We do not let him be pushed or crowded by the other dogs and we don't let him be exposed to individuals that might be afraid of him. What makes the difference for him is the ongoing, day-to-day structure that we provide. It calms him, defines his world for him and lets him know that we are keeping him safe. As a result, he is easy to manage and able to be the loving dog we knew he could be.

Reactive Behavior Toward External Triggers

We define reactive behaviors toward external triggers as reactiveness toward things outside of the dog's home environment. This includes other dogs, strangers, cars, hot air balloons, fireworks or anything else they alert to. Most of these reactions have their roots in inadequate early socialization. If for any reason dogs miss socialization to a wide range of specific triggers during their formative periods they can develop reactive behaviors towards unfamiliar stimuli. When this is combined with a heightened level of excitement, behaviors become unmanageable.

This is the most common form of reactive behavior, and although this is certainly an issue, it's generally the most straightforward form of reactive behavior to address. That doesn't make it easy, of course, just less challenging than other situations involving reactivity. Addressing these behaviors requires a sort of remedial education to help the dog learn the socialization they should have learned when they were young. They must be walked step-by-step through how to deal with their environment in a calm, healthy way. It takes time and patience, and an understanding that the dog needs to be set up to succeed.

Tools And Safety

In our experience, the most effective training tool for controlling reactive behaviors towards others in the moment it happens is a nose halter. When dealing with reactive behavior, we always have an additional long nylon slip training collar on the dog and we clip it and the nose halter together as an additional safety line. If the dog pulls the nose strap off, there should always be an additional tool on the dog that they can't slip out of.It needs to be long enough so that any guidance with the leash still occurs at the nose and does not pull at the neck.

We prefer this set-up because a nose halter does not cause pain, and it allows for turning the dog's head away from a problem and preventing eye contact. Try to find a trainer in your area that is comfortable training with a nose halter but without treats to teach you specific technique and help you deal with negative reactions.

A dog doesn't go from zero to lunge in one breath. There is a period of escalation the dog goes through when they encounter a trigger. First they glance, then they stare, then they fixate, then they lean in and lunge. It may happen in the space of a few fractions of a second, but the pattern is consistent. The earlier in that pattern the handler can redirect their line of sight away from the other dog or stranger, the easier it is to defuse the behavior before it gets out of hand.

Unfortunately, peoples' most common reaction when dogs act out is to panic, freeze and do nothing. Some people even forget to hang on to the leash. The simplest and most effective thing you can do in the moment a dog begins to act out is to move quickly away from whatever they are triggering at. Just turn and get away from the other dog or person. There will be a certain distance away at which the dog will begin to calm down and become more responsive to control again.

Dealing With External Triggers

So how do you actually make progress with reactive behavior towards external triggers such as dogs and strangers? As mentioned before, the dog needs to be given remedial education on how to have appropriate reactions they didn't learn as a puppy. To start with, you must have adequate control and good technique with the leash and nose halter. For reactive behavior we recommend finding a trainer with the appropriate skills and experience that will work with you privately. You will not likely make progress with reactive behavior in a class. It's disruptive in a group setting, and there are too many triggers at once for a dog to cope well. Find someone that will teach you individually, then practice in your home and yard. Be sure you can effectively control your dog when there are no triggers around before you attempt to take on the reactive behavior itself.

Once you feel you have good control in a contained environment, then find somewhere that has easy access to triggers the dog might act out at (dogs, traffic, etc.). Stay at least 50 – 80 yards away or more from the triggers initially. Only when your dog can consistently, reliably walk calmly with you at that distance do you begin to gradually move closer a little at a time. The objective is to build on success, so don't rush the process.

It will take repeated exposure at distance before you will likely see progress, so expect to go back over and over again. Don't get ahead of your dog's learning curve or your ability to handle them safely. If they get upset just turn their head away to break their line of sight, move a little farther away to calm them down then try again when they settle.

If possible, have an additional person with you as a spotter to help you ensure safety. If your dog gets reactive remember that the most important part is to hang on to the leash. If needed, you can have your spotter hang on to a long leash that is attached to a body harness (without tension on the leash) while you control the dog from the nose halter as an extra security against a large dog getting away from you. If you are being diligent with all the other pieces of the system presented in this book, with time and practice your dog will gradually become less reactive to the triggers until you can walk along the fence outside a dog park or around a parking lot without your dog acting out.

Good control and technique are required, but the most important element is the daily structure that creates calm. Remember that a social dog isn't so much a dog that can play with others, it's a dog that can leave others alone. All we need them to do is learn to disengage when asked. Don't get frustrated or impatient with the process. The dog didn't develop these behaviors in a day, and it's going to take more than a day to resolve them.

In-Fighting

Fighting within the home (pack-mates attacking each

other) can be a very challenging form of reactive behavior to address, since the stress trigger of the other dog is always present. It's tough to calm things down when the dogs are constantly tensing up and acting out at each other, and it requires ongoing, extensive supervision.

Before we discuss how to address in-fighting, there are a few points that are important:

- In-fighting usually starts and is propagated by an ongoing need for additional structure and guidance for appropriate behaviors.

Much of the conflict that occurs in homes could be avoided if the environment were more clearly regulated. When we receive a call about dogs fighting and we ask about the specific instances, the conversation often goes something like this: "Well, they always fight around the food bowls and he never lets her finish her meal, and the other day one of them had a bone and the other tried to take it and they started fighting, and last week I was just sitting with one of them in my lap petting her and she just looked at the other dog and he ran up and attacked her for no reason right on top of me!"

Having read the information presented earlier in this book, can you identify why that family would be having fights? They aren't regulating feeding, they are allowing the dogs on top of them, they are allowing them to hoard resources and they are allowing the dogs to stare at each other. Remember, staring is conflict. If a dog is on top of the human's lap receiving affection and is staring at another dog, the other dog will likely take it badly. It says to the other dog, "this is my human, I'm possessive of them, and they are giving me affection to affirm that I should feel this way."

- There are no good dogs and bad dogs when there is fighting in the house. Everyone participates in some way.

Even the old dog in the corner that wouldn't possibly cause problems and is always the target of the other dogs is participating in the tension in the home in some way. In many homes with in-fighting, the dog that is pulling out the teeth is not the dog that is antagonizing the situation. The other dogs create tension by staring, crowding, pushing, feeling possessive of the humans and otherwise being instigators until the problem dog acts out.

Why would a dog antagonize another? The most common reasons are poor socialization, miscommunication from the humans, and preferential treatment. To begin with, if a dog is not given appropriate socialization early in life they can have problems living peacefully with other animals. If a dog has missed good life lessons early on, the only option is to give them the skills they need. They need to be walked through the patterns of social behavior until they can perform them with confidence. This generally means using leashes and crates to ensure safety until routines are well-established.

More often, conflict occurs because the family isn't aware of how to fill the dogs' needs and regulate their behavior as discussed in previous chapters. As a consequence, the dogs develop unregulated attitudes, like children without a babysitter. They then turn that fussy, problematic attitude at each other. In addition to all of the routine and stability that is needed in every situation with conflict, dogs in this state of mind need to be engaged in structured activities that don't involve the other dog. Work activities need to be challenging and need to tap as much of each dog's potential as possible. Each dog's focus and interest has to be taken away from the other dog or conflict won't resolve.

Unintentional preferential treatment can also be a cause of conflict in the home. If one dog is allowed on the bed, on the furniture and is carried around while the other dogs aren't, none of them take it well. The dog receiving preferential treatment gets a big head and the ones that have more restrictive rules become uncooperative. To deal with conflict in the home, you must treat all the dogs the same. If the big dogs can't be on the furniture then the little dog needs to be on the floor as well. Since the big dogs can't be carried then the little dog needs to walk themselves around. Dogs clearly understand the concept of unfairness, and they won't settle down if one dog in the house is receiving preferential treatment. If you feel it would be unsafe for the little dog to be on the floor then institute a "crate and rotate" process until long-term solutions can be implemented.

- There is a concept that is necessary for behavioral re-habilitation: Be proactive, not reactive.

It's not sufficient to correct dogs after a fight has happened. The conflict already occurred and the behavi-or has been reinforced, regardless of how you respond after-the-fact. To learn stable behavior dogs have to be required to perform the desired patterns repetitively un-til they become habit. What is the desired behavior in a situation where dogs are fighting? Initially, to lay around quietly and leave each other alone. How can that be re-quired? With crates and leashes. This process is called "crate-and-rotate." You will need several cheap 4'-6' leashes, plenty of dog beds and at least one crate for each dog.

The idea is to teach the dogs how to lay together near each other, to function as a pack and to not fuss. In most situations there are two dogs that do the actual fighting and other dogs that will get along with either. Rotate through having the dogs that fight loose with the others, one at a time, with the other one in a crate for safety. Make sure that the dogs that don't fight also spend time crated so everyone is treated fairly. The objective is to break the group down into smaller, more manageable chunks so that relationships between the dogs can be addressed in a safe way. For this to be an effective approach, the dogs must be getting lots of exercise, time out of the crates in manageable groups, calm affection when their behavior warrants it, and a constant, never-ending sense of supervision from the humans.

Over time (measured in months, usually) as tensions slowly resolve the two dogs that have been fighting can be brought into gradually closer proximity while still on leash until they can lay near each other, but not so close they could have direct conflict. When crating the dogs, put the two with conflict in crates near each other. The more they are in close proximity without conflict the easier it gets for them to get along when loose together again.

As over time trust is developed in their reactions, supervised introductions between them on leash can be tried, in the yard without other dogs around. Walk them around until they are calm and ignoring each other. Bring one up to the other and let them sniff (nose to tail only) for a brief moment then separate them. Bring the other dog around to sniff then walk them around some more. Never let dogs you don't trust go nose-to-nose; it will likely go badly. If you see either of them tense up, turn away or try to put a nose or paw over the other dog, separate them immediately and walk them around some more before you try again.

Keep taking turns until both dogs can sit down with a, "yeah, I know what that dog smells like, already. Can we move on?" sort of attitude, then take them in and crate them next to each other again for awhile. After a few times doing this procedure if you feel you can trust them after they sniff and disengage you can let the leashes go and let them interact more naturally. If you see any tension begin to develop get hold of the leashes again quickly, separate them and walk them around some more and then go secure them. Remember to stay calm. Even when you feel you can safely have them together, do not leave them together unsupervised until they have really earned your trust.

In each situation with dogs that are fighting, the family

has to decide what level of reintegration they can be comfortable and successful with. Safety can be ensured in any environment if the family can be diligent with the "crate-and-rotate" procedure detailed above. It is not practical in every situation to move past that point. Even if the dogs can manage it, often the family can't step past their anxiety to allow the dogs loose again. "Crate-and-rotate" can be a viable long-term solution in many homes, and dogs are capable of thriving far more in even this restrictive of a situation than being re-homed or euthanized. Always work within the family's comfort zone for contact between the dogs.

What To Do If There Is A Fight

Let's be clear – there is NO safe way to break up a dog fight. We have rarely broken up a fight and not come away with some sort of injury, and how severe those injuries are each time is more a matter of luck than anything. Technique has very little to do with it. Attempt to directly intervene in a fight and there is a high probability of an injury of some sort. That being said, you can't just let them carry on. You have to find some way to break it up.

Our general advice for intervening in conflict is two-fold:

- The sooner you break things up the less drastic a measure that will be necessary to do so.

- Intervention should come from as far away as possible.

The longer dogs are allowed to maintain an attitude of conflict the more intense it gets. As they escalate, it takes correspondingly more direct intervention to stop them. Once intervention becomes necessary between dogs, it is best to approach the problem from as far away as is practical. Ideally, the family will be able to be diligent and catch the moment the dogs lock eyes. If they intervene at that point, before direct physical contact is made, the dogs can often be redirected with just a shout and a hand clap. Once they engage physically, more direct means are usually required to break it up. If that doesn't work, intervention should escalate in a steady fashion with the safest options attempted first.

If shouting is ineffective, water would normally be the next step of escalation. Get a hose and spray them or grab the dogs' water bowl and splash it on them to see if they disengage. This makes a mess, but still allows for intervention at a distance. The next level of escalation would be to try getting an object between them. Wedging a broom between, pushing a chair between them or blocking them with a briefcase or backpack are all viable options at this stage. Couch pillows can be good for separating smaller dogs.

At this point the humans are essentially in direct contact with the dog fight and the probability of personal injury rises dramatically. Almost any object in hand is better than nothing. The trash can, the baby's high chair, a laundry basket or whatever else may be handy can be the difference between whether the human is just shaken or wounded when the dust settles.

If dogs are prone to fighting and the methods mentioned previously aren't effective, a competent trainer needs to be brought in to coach the family through how to handle their dogs. Each situation is unique, and advice that is too generalized can be detrimental. Only, and we stress *only* if all other options have failed and you feel there is no other choice should you even consider engaging directly with your own body parts. There is no reliably safe way to do so. We know several techniques for directly handling challenging animals, and none of them work every time.

Despite best efforts, sometimes the worst occurs and there are no good options left. If you must intervene directly, there are a few points that can make a difference.

- As a general concept, the goal is to control each dog's

head at the base of the skull behind the ears by the scruff or collar to prevent the dog from turning to snap.

That sounds great in theory but can be tricky to implement when dogs are thrashing around. The most common result is that the dogs get in at least a random snap or two on a wrist while the human is trying to get a grip. Then there is that problematic moment when you find yourself holding two out of control dogs by the head and you don't know what to do next. The thing to do is secure them. Get one outside or into another room, then leash or crate the other.

- If there are two humans present each can grab the back legs of one of the dogs and wheel-barrow them backwards until they let go.

This is somewhat safer than controlling the head initially, but it's harder to get a leash on them once they are apart. If you just let go of them they'll likely go at each other again. If possible, use this to move them into separate spaces before dealing with leashes.

Understand clearly that once you cross the line of actually touching the dogs you are likely to pick up at least a minor bite of some kind, and the closer you are to the mouth when you touch the more likely it is to happen.

Cross the line of touching directly only in a case of last resort, and only if you feel you can definitively control the situation. It is very unsafe. We'd prefer to have more reassuring advice, but this is the reality of the situation. There is no safe way to touch fighting dogs. This is why we give a strong emphasis to our clients on using objects as buffers to direct physical contact.

Whatever happens, the family should NOT resort to hitting, kicking or beating the dogs. Those sorts of reactions are participating in the fight instead of resolving it. It will whip them into a frenzy beyond where they were and create a very real possibility that both dogs will turn on the human at once. Don't do it. Find some way to break it up that won't make things worse.

Once you manage to get the dogs apart, do not separate them for any longer than it takes to get both dogs secured. If there are two people present, get the dogs leashed then walk them around in the same space using the leashes with proper training halters for control to keep them from looking at each other until they calm down. Then, crate them next to each other and let them settle. If there is only one person present, go immediately to crating. This is extremely important.

The biggest mistake people make in this situation is to separate the dogs in different rooms. If you separate

SHELTER TO SERVICE DOG

them before they resolve the tensions they will engage at that level of conflict the next time they are together. This is how issues spiral out of control and families end up with dogs that can never be in the same space without fighting. Once a fight happens, expect at least 30-45 days of strict supervision before allowing them opportunities to earn your trust again.

A Word About Muzzles

Even in situations where dogs are having very reactive behaviors toward each other and the humans are afraid to intervene directly in conflict, there are often still negative reactions to the idea of using a muzzle as a tool to help maintain safety. To be plain, a muzzle is better than a vet bill or a law suit, and there must be some way of letting the dogs be loose together without worrying about their safety until they earn trust. Think of it as a crate for their nose. It's a tool that allows them increased freedom to roam and socialize, so when used properly it is a good thing.

There are two kinds of muzzles, and people often choose the wrong one when dealing with reactive dogs. First, there are cloth mesh muzzles like you might see your veterinarian use. These are only for use in situations where the dog will only be restrained for a few minutes.

They are not something for your dog to wear for hours on end. They are also not a good choice when dealing with reactive behaviors because the dog can still nip with their front teeth, but they can't open their mouth to pant or drink and can very easily overheat. People use them when they shouldn't because it is the more friendly-looking muzzle and people feel slightly better about it than the other options, even though it is not effective or healthy to use for extended periods.

The other kind of muzzle is called a "basket" or "cage" muzzle. These are actually the most gentle and effective form of muzzle for dealing with reactive issues. They provide full mouth coverage so the dog can't nip with their front teeth, they allow the dog to open their mouth sufficiently to pant and drink, and usually have nose pads and other features for comfort.

Basket muzzles are available with metal baskets or plastic baskets. Plastic muzzles are sometimes referred to as Greyhound muzzles. Greyhound muzzles are considered light-duty, and are usually sufficient if you more or less trust the dogs to not fight and just want an extra security against unforeseen mishaps. They are very light, easy for the dog to wear and are suitable for many situations. If a dog's behavior is severe then a more secure metal basket may be the better choice.

Socializing a dog to a basket muzzle is easy. Fold the straps out of the way, then let them eat kibble or treats out of it as if it were a bowl. Since we don't use treats for most training, wearing the muzzle quickly becomes a special treat for the dogs. Once they will stick their nose in easily, start to lift the strap over their head for just a moment as they eat then take it off again. Keep at it until they seem to be past any negative reactions to it. After that, clip the straps and leave it on for a moment, then take it off again. Keep at it until the dogs figure out that it's a good thing. Remember to wash it off before you let them around other dogs in it. Having some other dog trying to lick off the kibble residue while a dog is wearing the muzzle would be bad. Use the muzzles any time the dogs are loose together until you trust them completely.

Reactive Behavior Toward The Family

A dog that is reactive to it's family is a different thing to handle from a dog that acts out towards external triggers such as other dogs or strangers. If a dog is acting out at family members then competent, professional help should be called immediately, especially if anyone in the family has developed fear toward the dog. Never attempt to deal with a dog where safety is a concern without coaching and supervision.

The severity of the behavior should be taken into account when deciding how to respond to situations of a dog acting out at the family. Generally speaking, a dog that snaps out at the family but does not actually make contact or draw blood is not trying to hurt anyone. They are trying to set boundaries for others. It is the behavior of a dog that feels unsafe, and it requires a caring hand to address. Bear in mind, the dog may not have an intent for harm but it can certainly proceed to making contact if pushed past its comfort zones. Proceed slowly and gently when working with a fearful dog.

Dogs learn to snap and snarl as a result of being touched too much or in a way they find uncomfortable. At some point, they try growling and snapping as a response to feeling overwhelmed and when it works it becomes a tool in their toolkit to regulate their environment.

These behaviors are rooted in fear and personal space concerns. Dogs with these behaviors should be kept on leash next to an adult family member, then essentially ignored. Keep other pets or family members away, but allow the dog to acclimate to being near the human at their own pace. Periodically pass the dog to another family member, especially any they may be particularly nervous about. With time and patience the dog will build more trust, but don't try to "make friends" or push affection on the dog before they ask for it. It will overwhelm them and reinforce the fearful attitude.

If a dog is snapping out, always use leashes and safety gear that is appropriate for the dog's size. For a small dog that may be as simple as closed-toed shoes and a good pair of work gloves worn for handling drills and grooming. For dogs that are larger that may mean leather gauntlets (we use welding gloves) or a muzzle. Generally speaking, if a dog can't be handled completely safely with just a pair of work gloves then professional assistance is required. Protective gear does not prevent being bit or injured, it just helps minimize the damage. 15-20 lb. dogs have chewed on our hands with heavy leather gloves on and we've come away with extensive punctures, bruises and swelling. Granted, it was far better than it would have been otherwise, but that's small consolation in the moment.

If a dog snaps at you for any reason, get a leash and slide the clip through the handle to make a lasso. Loop the dog from arms-length while keeping your body parts out of the way. Do not try to touch them to clip their collar or get your hands near their face. Once you have hold of them with the lasso, move them away from where they were and walk them around to calm them down. After that you can release them if you wish or just keep them parked by your side.

A leash is the appropriate choice in almost all situations involving control with a dog you don't trust. Whatever the situation – they are on the couch and they growl at you, they jump on the bed and bark at you, they fuss over a toy – get a leash. Attach a leash before feeding for control and keep them on leash when company comes over. Remember to be diligent with the rest of the system presented here to establish control and calm as a daily pattern.

Mouthing Behaviors

Let's take a moment to differentiate "mouthing" from biting and aggression. Young dogs explore the world with their mouth and will often go through a stage where they try to put their mouth on everything and everyone. This is a normal, if annoying, stage in a puppy's development. Understand, this is not aggression or reactivity and a dog that puts it's mouth on you but never bites down and has a look in its eye like it is getting away with something and having fun at it is not likely to actually be a danger. Dogs never show restraint for what they intend. If they mean to hurt you they do, and it's immediate. They don't think, "I really want to hurt you but I won't. I'll just mouth at you instead." It doesn't really work that way.

It's best and easiest to deal with mouthing behaviors while a dog is still young. The one lesson a puppy should never learn is that their mouth can make people back away. For dogs under 6 months old, if they try to mouth at you the simplest thing to do is just hold their lower jaw. Do not squeeze or hurt them in any way, but hang on for a moment until they try to pull away from you, then let go while giving a verbal correction. After that, stick your hand out and give them the opportunity to mouth you again. Repeat the pattern until the dog does something besides mouthing, such as licking. The moment they do something more appropriate give them affection for it. Remember to stay calm at all times during this activity. If you get frustrated or angry it will encourage the behavior instead of deterring it.

This particular handling exercise is only for very young dogs. By the time a dog is 5-6 months old this will no longer help with the issue, it will just aggravate them.

For dogs that are over 5-6 months old we use verbal corrections and boundaries to deal with mouthing. The most important part of correcting older dogs is catching their moment of intent to mouth. Dogs aren't very subtle if you're paying attention. When they get that look in their eye that says, "I'm going for it, I'm gonna mouth you now" give a sharp verbal correction, stand up and back them away from you. If you don't see improvement within a short time or if it seems like the dog is escalating their behavior instead of calming down then get a leash and get professional help. Don't take chances if it seems like behavior is getting worse. As stated before, always find a competent trainer to work with you if you or anyone in your home doesn't feel safe around the dog or if you don't feel confident correcting them.

WHAT TO LOOK FOR IN A TRAINER

There is an old saying in the dog industry, "the only thing two trainers agree on is that the third one is lost." It's a world of conflicting advice, and at some point you have to pick someone to listen to. Choosing the right trainer to assist you can make all the difference in how things go in your home.

When looking for a trainer, especially if you need help dealing with reactive behavior in your dog, make sure they understand the importance of gentle handling in creating trust and safety. If they recommend a course of action that doesn't sound like it will make your dog feel more secure and safe but will suppress them, hurt them or cause additional fear then that person doesn't have a good understanding of the dog's needs and will likely make your issues worse rather than better.

The same is true if they try to deal with reactive or problem behavior by excessively "treating" the dog. Many trainers try to use either aversion training or strict operant conditioning to address reactive and problem behaviors, and neither approach is particularly effective (aversion training is a form of operant conditioning as well, but for our purposes we will separate them).

Aversion Training

Aversion training, also called "force methods", usually involves choke chains, prong collars or shock collars, and the basic idea is to cause discomfort to the dog until they taper off a behavior from an aversion to the unpleasant consequence. Trainers that advocate these methods explain it in other ways to couch it in warm fuzzy feelings, but regardless of how it is described, the methods are inherently violent.

Before you put a device of that sort on your dog, wrap it around your own neck and have them yank it the way they want to yank on your dog. Sounds preposterous on the face of it, doesn't it? Why don't you want some stranger to put a prong collar or chain around your neck and yank on it over and over? Because you know perfectly well it will hurt you badly. Don't do to your dog something you are unwilling to do to yourself. On that point, shock collars really do cause pain. Trainers that use them often try to explain the horrible yowl the dog makes as the collar simply stimulating the dog's vocal cords, but that's not the situation. The dog really is in pain.

So how will any of that sort of thing make your dog less afraid and more stable and trusting? Obviously it won't. Don't do it no matter how sure of themselves the trainer may seem. Training methods are something trainers get very territorial over and those that disagree do so vehemently, but for us it's not about the dogs or the effectiveness of the technique, it's about who we are as people. We simply aren't willing to use force or cause pain to an animal for convenience. Our sense of decency won't allow it from us. Each person must decide for themselves whether they are willing to hurt an animal for their own purposes. It's an individual choice, but we feel it defines something fundamental about who we are as individuals. It doesn't matter whether it works or not. It's cruel.

Operant Conditioning

Operant conditioning is based on the idea that behavior (particularly in animals) is primarily a function of reward and punishment. It is the idea behind treat training and other forms of reinforcement obedience training. While it is true that animals can be taught specific behaviors through the application of food reward, this is not helpful when dealing with reactive behavior in dogs. In a controlled training environment there is no other motivator other than the reward or punishment, so an animal will respond in predictable ways. When addressing reactive behavior, the dog's fear in the moment, level of excitement, their instincts as predatory pack animals and their feelings of possessiveness of the owner due to lack of structure are also powerful motivating factors that make simple reward / punishment response patterns unclear and ineffective.

While not detrimental in the way aversion training is, using food rewards to redirect a dog also tends to make reactive behavior worse rather than better. Remember that food always rewards the state of mind and actions the dog has in the moment the food is received (this is the basis of using food as reward in operant conditioning). It doesn't change anything, it just reinforces. When handlers attempt to use food to bait a dog out of reactive behavior it simply reinforces the negative state of mind rather than redirecting it. Even if the dog learns to turn their nose away, they have not calmed down at all from the trigger before food is applied. Food has no place in dealing with reactiveness and aggression.

Most of all, remember that a dog isn't just a bundle of conditioned responses. It is an intelligent, sensitive creature that is capable of communicating with and responding to its environment. You will never resolve behavioral issues until you resolve the underlying stresses that are motivating the behavior, which usually boils down to lack of structure in their day-to-day life. Reactions must be regulated in the moment that they occur, but the reactions will not stop until the underlying stress is addressed.

FROM SHELTER TO SERVICE DOG

CONCLUSION

So there you have it. Everything you need to know to address most issues with your dogs and guide them into being healthy, well-adjusted members of society. It's a lot to take in at first, and you may need to read this more than once to really have all the concepts click, but be diligent. Every part of the information we've presented here is important so take the time to implement it all. Most of all remember that these are not things that we do to fix a problem then quit when the dog is "better." These patterns must be kept in place for the life of the dog for long-term success. Be patient, be consistent and stay calm and you will be well on your way to having a happy, satisfying relationship with your dog.